SO-AFJ-428

50

> For most of human history,
> to be able to live without work
> has been considered
> the most fortunate lot of man.
> Work was the curse of Adam,
> and to be relieved of it
> was not only counted a blessing
> but commanded universal respect
> of the individual so blessed. . . .
>
> —J.R.L. Anderson

Man AGAINST Work

edited by
Lloyd Zimpel

William B. Eerdmans Publishing Company

© 1974 William B. Eerdmans Pub. Co.
All Rights Reserved

Printed in the U.S.A.

Library of Congress Cataloging in Publication Data

Zimpel, Lloyd, comp.
  Man against work.

  CONTENTS: Fenton, P. Confessions of a working stiff.—Hart, H.
Factory girl.—Kremen, B. No pride in this dust. [etc.]

  L. Labor and laboring classes—United States—
1970-   —Addresses, essays, lectures. 2. Work—
Addresses, essays, lectures. I. Title.

HD8072.Z54   301.5'5   74-8126

ISBN 0-8028-1584-7

Contents

6

Man Against Work

Introduction:
The Curse of Adam

Readers acquainted with the noted essays by Harvey Swados, "The Myth of the Happy Worker," and Daniel Bell, "Work and its Discontents," will see that these two seminal pieces lay the field for many of the contributions to this book. Indeed, the titles in themselves predicted the nature of the scrutiny the American worker would receive in the two decades following the mid-1950s when Swados and Bell wrote.*

It was in those languid Eisenhower years that many of us, adrift between the military draft and stabs at college for which we were badly equipped, found ourselves repeating the mistakes of our fathers and haphazardly slipping toward that myth and its discontents. With old high-school mates and ex-Army privates I found myself working at random jobs in foundry, meat-packing plant, refrigerator assembly line. Some sort of ridiculous mistake had put us there, we were all sure, and we swapped lies about how we'd soon be quitting for first-rate junior executive slots at, say, 3M. That the foundry coreroom or the freezer line amounted to the sum of one's ambition was unthinkable, even though we knew in a vague way that we probably weren't suited for jobs that took less muscle, commanded more money, and were more fun to do. If we felt anything for our jobs it was contempt. At one time in the foundry coreroom we sweated for weeks at a gritty, high-speed job, where there wasn't time

---

*"The Myth of the Happy Worker" is reprinted in Swados' *A Radical's America*, Atlantic-Little, Brown, 1962. "Work and its Discontents" was reprinted as a booklet by The League for Industrial Democracy in 1970.

to go to the toilet except during rest periods, making oddly shaped sand castings with no idea of what they were for. "Something for tractor transmissions," someone guessed. It underscored our sense of the worthlessness of the work not to find out — or at least not to admit we cared. How poor one's life must be if *this* counted! It didn't matter; it was all a joke. We traded time for money in a transaction of existential absurdity. Soon we'd be on to better things and life would begin.

The older workers we regarded with condescension. Many of them had worked, or wanted to, through the Depression and now labored without complaint, still relishing overtime as a treat. But many other workers were only a few years beyond us. The sluggards hadn't flown when they could — we figured everyone had the option to flee. Wise in our youth and unencumbered by expense of family, car payments, beer and liquor costs (an overwhelming outlay for many workers), we knew that somehow we would escape the trap.

Some of us did; but some didn't and in another year or two the jaws of the trap closed on them: life was not going to begin. Of those who stayed, many felt they must suffer boring jobs in order to support the families they, willy-nilly, had started to raise. Some found diversion enough in weekend boozing, or in working around the tract houses their wives' jobs and their own weary moonlighting eventually helped buy. But others were openly bitter and resented the pointlessness of their jobs and thus their lives. With a worker's apocalypse nowhere in sight they swallowed their discontent or expressed it through conventional and not always serviceable union channels. It would not be until nearly twenty years later that workers of their mood, but of another more self-assured generation, would find a new militant voice. As it was, their dissatisfaction, however angry and despairing, remained individual and veiled. They punched in for each shift as if it were an eight-hour sentence; and this, it was their desperate understanding, they would do for the rest of their working lives.

In no era, one suspects, did the work ethic grip the

American worker as tightly as we now wistfully declare, although whatever hold it did have loosened greatly in the past two decades. During that time in America technological advances, crash education programs, and exposure to torrents of information through the mass media all speeded a general change in values and environment. Such influences altered the expectations of workers too, but did not always correspondingly alter the nature of their work, and from this unhappy discrepancy grew the "myth" that Swados noted. It was a myth propounded by intellectuals who, sourly eyeing the worker's mundane aspirations, claimed he had grown "fat, satisfied, smug, a little restless but hardly distinguishable from his fellow TV-viewers of the middle-class." He no longer fit the intellectual's vision of the worker as an heroic figure striding out of the 1930s and 40s to build a new society. Because he sought "barbecue pits more than foreign aid and air-conditioning more than desegregation" the myth took hold among non-workers that the worker was fat and happy. Unnoticed or ignored was the fact that his job was still as stultifying and degrading as ever, and that he still approached it daily with "hatred, shame and resignation."

The realistic appraisals of work and the worker by Swados and Bell and subsequent writers confirmed the suspicion of workers that dull, hard work is not ennobling; it does not make heroes. That seems obvious to the 70s, but twenty years ago we were less sure. Now we know that there is little in assembly-line or dead-end paper-work jobs that a man can identify as a worthy extension of himself; such work is more likely to shame and humiliate him. Work systems rising from "the cult of efficiency," Bell pointed out in "Work and its Discontents," offend the worker's welfare and dignity. A man's job "must not only feed his body; it must sustain his spirit." Today we assent to this, as we are also ready to believe that work in general is not the single or most favorable means to fortify one's spirit. Nor is it through work that one best justifies himself in the eyes of his fellows. Young workers no longer pretend that it is; and such disenchantment is not limited only to the blue-collar young: a 1973 survey showed that four out of five American business-

men, that least starry-eyed of classes, no longer defined personal success in terms of work.

Today's young worker comes to assembly line or office
desk well schooled in militancy by recent events that have
loudly trumpeted underdog causes to the world. If the 70s
prove to be the worker's decade for dissent, he can find
congenial models in a variety of movements in the 60s: students, from the Berkeley free-speech era to the Columbia
University trashers; civil rights marchers, black militants,
draft resisters; welfare rights workers; political direct action-
ists; prison reformers; gay liberationists; feminists. These
multiple influences merge into an aggressive spirit of the
times which invades factory and office at virtually every
level. At one time it may show itself in such old-fashioned
combative ways as the 1972 Lordstown General Motors strike,
which resulted when young workers protested assembly-line
speed-ups. At other times it may take newer forms, as occurred
in the summer of 1973 when defiant workers seized a Chrysler
plant in Detroit. The specific grievances leading to this
short-lived takeover were less remarkable than the fact that
the rebellion of the young, largely black — and, almost in-
cidentally, politically leftist — leadership shattered another
tradition, that of the employee-union-management relationship as the end-all for settling employee disputes. An extensive network of rigid union rules for pursuing grievances was
not so much circumvented as trampled on. Management and
old-line union officials alike offered up public prayers that
the action of the young Detroit rebels, reminiscent of student
militancy in the 60s, hadn't set a precedent and made such
fierce heterodoxy a new form of rank-and-file action.

But as threatening as worker militancy is to uneasy
managers, it does not herald revolution in every display.
Frequently it reveals itself in unexceptional ways: employees
have become more "verbal and articulate" over the past five
years a national personnel survey found in 1973, noting also
that a change in the character of the worker has required
employers to stiffen some rules regarding drugs and relax
others concerning proper dress — and scrap altogether sus-

pensions from work as being no real punishment since "many employees welcome time off, particularly when the weather is good." A far cry from my foundry colleagues who greeted overtime as a prize.

Most of the articles here draw in part on common underlying themes and concepts about the nature of work and the worker's lot. Some of these ideas, such as worker "alienation," or "job enrichment" as a solution to worker discontent, are plainly set forth. Others, understood but not always spelled out, also contribute to the shape of the worker's world:

Taylorism. Frederick Winslow Taylor's turn-of-the-century doctrine of scientific management and time-and-motion studies set standards of assembly-line efficiency always mistrusted by the worker. Lately they have come into question by some of the people who once applied them.

The Great Depression. The grim 1930s taught an older American generation to revere work as essential to security, thus scaring it into everlasting anxiety over prospects of unemployment. However, that same era holds no power over those born into the affluence which followed.

The Protestant or Work Ethic. Certain religious and moral traditions suggest that man is justified before God, his family, and himself principally by the work he does. Salvation, at least in part, lies in keeping busy, deferring gratification, and recognizing authority. Work, then, is not the curse of Adam but a Divine summons to earthly esteem. There exists as well an American sub-ethic honoring work as a badge of personal identification, although this carries little weight outside of professional circles and even there is fading in importance.

Liberation Movements. A number of highly publicized movements have supplied models for worker dissent, and have influenced it otherwise as well. (For that matter, the worker's plight has also shaped certain popular movements, *viz.*, encounter groups with their predominance of alienated workers in obsessive search for the fulfillment denied them in their jobs.) The woman's movement, for example, has had particular impact upon male willingness to suffer unpleasant work simply because it was accepted custom that such personal sacrifices were required to provide for the family. As Daniel Yankelovich points out, now that women are "more economically assertive and independent," the man's role as bread-winner has diminished and he is less willing to endure degrading labor if his sacrifice goes unappreciated.

Foreign Competition; Labor Costs. On the one hand the foreign experience is useful in shaming indolent Americans: Japanese workers, for example, are said to abhor absenteeism, regard work as a virtue, and, despite minuscule fringe benefits, loyally sing company songs and perform self-improving calisthenics during lunch-hours. On the other hand European experiments to benefit the worker far outreach those undertaken by U.S. employers, who plead high labor costs as a barrier: Richard C. Gerstenberg, General Motors chairman, says that any "shortening or rearrangement of the work week that will give the employee greater leisure time or . . . greater control over the hours and pattern of his work . . . threatens to increase the cost of labor . . . which must invariably be reflected in the price of the product."

Worker Resentment. Many of the older generation of workers are severely piqued by the demands of their juniors. "Indignation and even rage . . . are aroused in the breasts of those whose lives have been suffused by and subordinated to the work ethic at the prospect that anybody else may be given a better chance in life than they had," notes Edgar Z. Friedenberg. He cites a report from *Work in America* about an experiment in a Norwegian metalworking plant designed to improve the worker's circumstances: "Production increased so much due to job redesign that the experiment was suspended: the unskilled workers in the experiment had begun to take home pay packets in excess of the most skilled workers in the firm, thus engendering bitterness."

Pride of Workmanship. Usually invoked for its absence, a worker's pride draws largely upon his certainty of, and ability to observe, the social utility of what he does. Robert Sherrill writes that "even the dumbest worker hired to manufacture spray deodorant containers . . . must realize that it wouldn't really matter if his factory closed down forever. So why should he care about his work? . . . Until we get rid of products that aren't worth killing ourselves over there's something to be said for the milder forms of sabotage, such as that of one steelworker who confessed that 'when I make something, I put a little dent in it. I like to do something to make it really unique.' "

It is unlikely that the steelworker with his creative urge will serve as the ultimate model for the nonconforming young work force of the 70s; but it is in part this impulse toward invention, this insistence upon making one's mark and asserting individuality in one's work that has caught the attention of the social scientists. The failure of the work world to engage this impulse and individuality is of concern to them too, as reflected throughout this book. Recently, such massive studies as those conducted by the University of Michigan Survey Research Center, and the report *Work in America,* commissioned by the U.S. Department of Health, Education, and Welfare — sections of which are reprinted here — provide the surety of graphs and statistics to the earlier perceptions of Swados and Bell. By the very extent of their data these later studies imply that they hold something of immediate utility as well — answers to the manager's always practical question: if we admit worker discontent then how do we deal with it?

The answers that emerge to such workaday problems are equivocal. Do we woo the alienated worker by broadening the scope of his responsibilities on the job? Or is this, as several writers here suggest, largely an anti-union ploy which, like the much-discussed four-day week, tends to benefit the corporation more than the worker? Should the worker have a voice in electing his own foremen and executives? Will letting him set his own hours do the trick? European companies have taken steps to find out, some of them recounted in the concluding essay in this book, but how far along similar paths American employers are willing to go is still undetermined. Nor is it yet assured that job enrichment or similar programs, even widely applied, will indeed penetrate to the root of worker protest. Their failure to do so can only bring on the question of whether true remedies lie anywhere within the present work structure — a nettlesome but persistent question that occurred in a political framework in earlier decades and returns now in a broader social context. We are only now admitting the sense of such a notion, worker militancy having lent it sudden relevance, and just beginning to puzzle through the information that may yet lead to new proposals for radically altering the force and purpose of work in our lives.

When those proposals are finally made, they will doubtless depend much upon the issues and inquiries brought forward by the contributors to this book, regarding new influences, displaced aspirations, transformed values, the shifting economic, moral, and political pressures of the 1970s, all those currents that have washed away the "happy" myth and set before us the youthful worker as he persists in being seen today, in a deepening temper of protest and discontent.

— L.Z.

Contributors

IVAR BERG is professor of sociology and business at Columbia University and the author of *Values in a Business Society, The Business of America,* and *Education and Jobs: The Great Training Robbery.*

THOMAS R. BROOKS, a labor historian, is the author of *Toil and Trouble.*

LEWIS CARLINER, professor of labor studies at Rutgers University, worked for many years in the education program of the United Auto Workers.

DENNIS DERRYCK, president of a social research firm, also teaches urban education and manpower policy at Brandeis University.

THOMAS H. FITZGERALD is director of employee research and training at the Chevrolet Division of General Motors Corporation.

NATHAN GLASSMAN is a manager with the Linde Division of Union Carbide Corporation.

WILLIAM GOMBERG is an industrial engineer and professor of industrial relations at the Wharton School of Finance of the University of Pennsylvania.

JUDSON GOODING, a former editor of *Fortune* Magazine, is the author of *The Job Revolution.*

JOHN S. GREENEBAUM is an attorney in Louisville, Kentucky, specializing in labor-management relations.

JOHN HAYNES is the community action director for District 3 of the International Union of Electrical, Radio and Machine Workers.

JANICE NEIPERT HEDGES is an economist with the U.S. Bureau of Labor Statistics.

JOAN JORDAN is a San Francisco free-lance writer and researcher on the economic aspects of women's liberation.

BENNETT KREMEN has contributed to the *New York Times* and *Village Voice*. His article here is in part the first chapter of his new book *Dateline: America,* Dial Press, 1974.

R. J. KRICKUS teaches political science at Mary Washington University and is the author of the forthcoming book *White Ethnic Politics: Reaction or Populism.*

JEROME M. ROSOW is a former assistant secretary in the U. S. Department of Labor.

ROBERT SCHRANK, a consultant on manpower programs, was formerly deputy manpower commissioner of the City of New York.

DANIEL ZWERDLING is a free-lance writer in Washington, D.C.

PART ONE

Eight Hours a Day, Five Days a Week

Confessions of a Working Stiff

by Patrick Fenton

The Big Ben is hammering out its 5:45 alarm in the half-dark of another Tuesday morning. If I'm lucky, my car down the street will kick over for me. I don't want to think about that now; all I want to do is roll over into the warm covers that hug my wife. I can hear the wind as it whistles up and down the sides of the building. Tuesday is always the worst day—it's the day the drudgery, boredom, and fatigue start all over again. I'm off from work on Sunday and Monday, so Tuesday is my blue Monday.

I make my living humping cargo for Seaboard World Airlines, one of the big international airlines at Kennedy Airport. They handle strictly all cargo. I was once told that one of the Rockefellers is the major stockholder for the airline, but I don't really think about that too much. I don't get paid to think. The big thing is to beat that race with the time clock every morning of your life so the airline will be happy. The worst thing a man could ever do is to make suggestions about building a better airline. They pay people $40,000 a year to come up with better ideas. It doesn't matter that these ideas never work, it's just that they get nervous when a guy from South Brooklyn or Ozone Park acts like he actually has a brain.

I throw a Myadec high-potency vitamin into my mouth to ward off one of the ten colds I get every year from humping mailbags out in the cold rain at Kennedy. A huge DC-8 stretch jet waits impatiently for the 8,000 pounds of mail that I will soon feed its empty belly. I wash the Myadec down

Reprinted with the permission of *New York* Magazine.
Copyright © 1973 by the NYM Corp.

with some orange juice and grab a brown bag filled with bologna and cheese. Inside the lunch bag there is sometimes a silly note from my wife that says, "I Love You—Guess Who?" It is all that keeps me going to a job that I hate.

I've been going there for seven years now and my job is still the same. It's weary work that makes a man feel used up and worn out. You push and you pull all day long with your back. You tie down pallets loaded with thousands of pounds of freight. You fill igloo-shaped containers with hundreds of boxes that all look the same. If you're assigned to work the warehouse, it's really your hard luck. This is the job all the men hate most. You stack box upon box until the pallet resembles the exact shape of the inside of the plane. You get the same monotonous feeling an adult gets when he plays with a child's blocks. When you finish one pallet, you find another and start the whole dull process over again.

The airline pays me $192 a week for this. After they take out taxes and $5.81 for the pension, I go home with $142. Once a month they take out $10 for term life insurance, and $5.50 for union dues. The week they take out the life insurance is always the worst: I go home with $132. My job will never change. I will fill up the same igloos with the same boxes for the next 34 years of my life, I will hump the same mailbags into the belly of the plane, and push the same 8,000-pound pallets with my back. I will have to do this until I'm 65 years old. Then I'll be free, if I don't die of a heart attack before that, and the airline will let me retire.

In winter the warehouse is cold and damp. There is no heat. The large steel doors that line the warehouse walls stay open most of the day. In the cold months, wind, rain and snow blow across the floor. In the summer the warehouse becomes an oven. Dust and sand from the runways mix with the toxic fumes of fork lifts, leaving a dry, stale taste in your mouth. The high windows above the doors are covered with a thick, black dirt that kills the sun. The men work in shadows with the constant roar of jet engines blowing dangerously in their ears.

Working the warehouse is a tedious job that leaves a man's mind empty. If he's smart he will spend his days woolgathering. He will think about pretty girls that he once knew, or some other daydream of warm, dry places where you never had a chill. The worst thing he can do is to think about his problems. If he starts to think about how he is going to pay the mortgage on the $30,000 home that he can't afford, it will bring him down. He will wonder why he comes to the cargo airline every morning of his life, and even on Christmas Day. He will start to wonder why he has to listen to the deafening sound of the jets as they rev up their engines. He will wonder why he crawls on his hands and knees, breaking his back a little bit more every day.

To keep his kids in that great place in the country in the summer, that great place far away from Brooklyn and the South Bronx, he must work every hour of overtime that the airline offers him. If he never turns down an hour, if he works some 600 hours over, he can make about $15,000. To do this he must turn against himself, he must pray that the phone rings in the middle of the night, even though it's snowing out and he doesn't feel like working. He must hump cargo late into the night, eat meatball heroes for supper, drink coffee that starts to taste like oil, and then hope that his car starts when it's time to go home. If he gets sick — well, he'd better not think about that.

All over Long Island, Ozone Park, Brooklyn, and as far away as the Bronx, men stir in the early morning hours as a new day begins. Every morning is the same as the last. Some of the men drink beer for breakfast instead of coffee. Way out in Bay Shore a cargoman snaps open a can of Budweiser. It's 6 a.m., and he covers the top of the can with his thumb in order to keep down the loud hiss as the beer escapes. He doesn't want to awaken his children as they dream away the morning in the next room. Soon he will swing his Pinto wagon up onto the crowded Long Island Expressway and start the long ride to the job. As he slips the car out of the driveway he tucks another can of beer between his legs.

All the men have something in common: they hate the work they are doing and they drink a little too much. They come to work only to punch a timecard that has their last name on it. At the end of the week they will pick up a paycheck with their last name on it. They will never receive a bonus for a job well done, or even a party. At Christmastime a card from the president of the airline will arrive at each one of their houses. It will say Merry Christmas and have the president's name printed at the bottom of it. They know that the airline will be there long after they are dead. Nothing stops it. It runs non-stop, without sleep, through Christmas Day, New Year's Eve, Martin Luther King's birthday, even the deaths of Presidents.

It's seven in the morning and the day shift is starting to drift in. Huge tractors are backed up to the big-mouth doors of the warehouse. Cattle trucks bring tons of beef to feed its insatiable appetite for cargo. Smoke-covered trailers with refrigerated units packed deep with green peppers sit with their diesel engines idling. Names like White, Mack, and Kenworth are welded to the front of their radiators, which hiss and moan from the overload. The men walk through the factory-type gates of the parking lot with their heads bowed, oblivious of the shuddering diesels that await them.

Once inside the warehouse they gather in groups of threes and fours like prisoners in an exercise yard. They stand in front of the two time clocks that hang below a window in the manager's office. They smoke and cough in the early morning hour as they await their work assignments. The manager, a nervous-looking man with a stomach that is starting to push out at his belt, walks out with the pink work sheets in his hand.

Eddie, a young Irishman with a mustache, has just bolted in through the door. The manager has his timecard in his hand, holding it so no one else can hit Eddie in. Eddie is four minutes late by the time clock. His name will now go down in the timekeeper's ledger. The manager hands the card to him with a "you'll be up in the office if you don't straighten out" look. Eddie takes the card, hits it in, and slowly takes his place with the rest of the men. He has been out till four in the morning drinking beer in the bars of Ozone Park: the time clock and the manager could blow up, for all he cares. "Jesus," he says to no one in particular, "I hope to Christ they don't put me in the warehouse this morning."

Over in another group, Kelly, a tall man wearing a navy knit hat, talks to the men. "You know, I almost didn't make it in this morning. I passed this green VW on the Belt Parkway. The girl driving it was singing. Jesus, I thought to myself, it must be great going somewhere at 6:30 in the morning that makes you want to sing." Kelly is smiling as he talks. "I often think, why the hell don't you keep on going, Kelly? Don't get off at the cargo exit, stay on. Go anywhere, even if it's only Brooklyn. Christ, if I was a single man I think I would do just that. Some morning I'd pass this damn place by and drive as far away as Riverhead. I don't know what I'd do when I got there — maybe I'd pick up a pound of beefsteak tomatoes from one of those roadside stands or something."

The men laugh at Kelly but they know he is serious. "I feel the same way sometimes," the man next to him says. "I find myself daydreaming a lot lately; this place drives you to that. I get up in the morning and I just don't want to come to work. I get sick when I hit that parking lot. If it wasn't for the kids and the house I'd quit." The men then talk about how hard it is to get work on "the outside." They mention "outside" as if they were in a prison.

Each morning there is an Army-type roll call from the leads. The leads are foremen who must keep the men moving; if they don't, it could mean their jobs. At one time they had power over the men but as time went by the company took away their little bit of authority. They also lost the deep interest, even enjoyment, for the hard work they once did. As the cargo airline grew, it beat this out of them, leaving only apathy. The ramp area is located in the backyard of the warehouse. This is where the huge jets park to unload their 70,000-pound payloads. A crew of men fall in behind the ramp lead as he mopes out of the warehouse. His long face shows the hopelessness of another day.

A brutal rain has started to beat down on the oil-covered concrete of the ramp as the 306 screeches in off the runway. Its engines scream as they spit off sheets of rain and oil.

Two of the men cover their ears as they run to put up a ladder to the front of the plane. The airline will give them ear covers only if they pay for half of them. A lot of the men never buy them. If they want, the airline will give them two little plugs free. The plugs don't work and hurt the inside of the ears.

The men will spend the rest of the day in the rain. Some of them will set up conveyor belts and trucks to unload the thousands of pounds of cargo that sit in the deep belly of the plane. Then they will feed the awkward bird until it is full and ready to fly again. They will crawl on their hands and knees in its belly, counting and humping hundreds of mailbags. The rest of the men will work up topside on the plane, pushing 8,000-pound pallets with their backs. Like Egyptians building a pyramid, they will pull and push until the pallet finally gives in and moves like a massive stone sliding through sand. They don't complain too much; they know that when the airline comes up with a better system some of them will go.

The old-timers at the airline can't understand why the younger men stay on. They know what the cargo airline can do to a man. It can work him hard but make him lazy at the same time. The work comes in spurts. Sometimes a man will be pushed for three hours of sweat, other times he will just stand around bored. It's not the hard work that breaks a man at the airline, it's the boredom of doing the same job over and over again.

At the end of the day the men start to move in off the ramp. The rain is still beating down at their backs but they move slowly. Their faces are red and raw from the rain-soaked wind that has been snapping at them for eight hours. The harsh wind moves in from the direction of the city. From the ramp you can see the Manhattan skyline, gray- and blue-looking, as it peeks up from the west wall of the warehouse. There is nothing to block the winter weather as it rolls in like a storm across a prairie. They head down to the locker room, heads bowed, like a football team that never wins.

With the workday almost over, the men move between the narrow, gray rows of lockers. Up on the dirty walls that surround the lockers someone has written a couple of four-letter words. There is no wit to the words; they just say the usual. As they strip off their wet gear the men seem to come alive.

"Hey, Arnie! You want to stay four hours? They're asking for overtime down in Export," one of the men yells over the lockers.

Arnie is sitting about four rows over, taking off his heavy winter clothing. He thinks about this for a second and yells back, "What will we be doing?"

"Working the meat trailer." This means that Arnie will be humping huge sides of beef off rows of hooks for four hours. Blood will drip down onto his clothes as he struggles to the front of the trailer. Like most of the men, he needs the extra money, and knows that he should stay. He has Master Charge, Korvettes, Times Square Stores, and Abraham & Straus to pay.

"Nah, I'm not staying tonight. Not if it's working the meat trailer. Don wanted to stop for a few beers at The Owl; maybe I'll stay tomorrow night."

It's four o'clock in the afternoon now — the men have twelve minutes to go before they punch out. The airline has stopped for a few seconds as the men change shifts. Supervisors move frantically across the floor pushing the fresh lot of new men who have just started to come in. They hand out work sheets and yell orders: "Jack, get your men into their rain gear. Put three men in the bellies to finish off the 300 flight. Get someone on the pepper trailers, they've been here all morning."

The morning shift stands around the time clock with three minutes to go. Someone says that Kevin Delahunty has just been appointed to the Fire Department. Kevin, a young Irishman from Ozone Park, has been working the cargo airline for six years. Like most of the men, he has hated every minute of it. The men are openly proud of him as they reach out to shake his hand. Kevin has found a job on "the outside." "Ah, you'll be leaving soon," he tells Pat. "I never thought I'd get out of here either, but you'll see, you're going to make it."

The manager moves through the crowd handing out timecards and stops when he comes to Kevin. Someone told him Kevin is leaving. "Is that right, Delahunty? Well, I guess we won't expect you in tomorrow, will we? Going to become a fireman, eh? That means you'll be jumping out of windows like a crazy man. Don't act like you did around here," he adds as he walks back to his office.

The time clock hits 4:12 and the men pour out of the warehouse. Kevin will never be back, but the rest of them will return in the morning to grind out another eight hours. Some of them will head straight home to the bills, screaming children, and a wife who tries to understand them. They'll have a Schaefer or two, then they'll settle down to a night of *The Courtship of Eddie's Father, The Rookies, Here's Lucy,* and the late news.

Some of them will start to fill up the cargo bars that surround Kennedy Airport. They will head to places like Gaylor's on Rockaway Boulevard or The Dew Drop Inn down near Farmers Boulevard. They will drink deep glasses of whiskey and cold mugs of Budweiser. The Dew Drop has a honky-tonk mood of the Old West to it. The barmaid moves around like a modern-day Katie Elder. Like Brandy, she's a fine girl, but she can out-curse any cargoman. She wears a low-cut blouse that reveals most of her breasts. The jukebox will beat out some Country & Western as she says, "Ah, hell, you played my song." The cargomen will hoot and holler as she substitutes some of her own obscene lyrics.

They will drink late into the night, forgetting time clocks, Master Charge, First National City, Korvettes, mortgages, cars that don't start, and jet engines that hurt their ears. They will forget about damp, cold warehouses, winters that get longer and colder every year, minutes that drift by like hours, supervisors that harass, and the thought of growing old on a job they hate. At midnight they will fall dangerously into their cars and make their way up onto the Southern State Parkway. As they ride into the dark night of Long Island they will forget it all until 5:45 the next morning — when the Big Ben will start up the whole grind all over again.

Factory Girl

by Holly Hart

Last winter I was a factory worker at Omark Industries in Oregon.

There was one young woman in our department who had been put in charge of the plastics section. She was a good worker, fast and skilled at showing new women the ropes.

Her family had been too poor to send her to college. Since high school she had worked at half a dozen unskilled jobs. After she had perfected her work at each one and seen that there was no chance of being promoted to more interesting work, she would move on to another job to escape the numbing boredom.

Then at Omark she thought at last she might have a chance. The foreman noticed how smart she was and made her lead-girl in plastics. It wasn't a real promotion for it brought no raise. It just gave her a break from regular, monotonous production work: she had a few supervisory responsibilities that meant she didn't have to spend the whole day sitting in the same place doing the same thing.

A lot of changes were being made in the department. There were always engineers around, collecting information to design new equipment and try out new production techniques. Once a large order of parts had to be scrapped because of defects. The engineers scurried around trying to figure out what had gone wrong.

She looked over the bad parts, examined the forms, and molds and tools, and spotted what was going wrong. This

Reprinted with permission. Copyright © 1971 by *Women: A Journal of Liberation,* 3028 Greenmount Ave., Baltimore, Md.

sort of thing kept happening. She also asked a lot of questions whenever an engineer was around and pretty soon she was being consulted on a lot of things.

As the department grew, there was a need for a production scheduler. The foreman put her to work designing a scheduling system and he planned on giving her the job as soon as things were ready to go.

But then the no-no came down from the higher-ups. The job was given to a man in the department. After he bungled it, we all expected that the bosses would wake up and give it back to her. After all, she had already shown she could do the job well.

But then it was announced that the job was being given to another man. To top it off, this was one of the worst guys in the department. He was always making dirty cracks at the women while we worked. Or he would ignore us when we needed something, basking in his supervisory self-importance. Now he was being promoted and we would have to put up with even more from him!

This was such a clear case of discrimination against a woman that, as we talked among ourselves, some of us decided to go to the foreman and ask him not only why she wasn't being given the job, but also how women could get ahead within the department and in the company. Male unskilled production workers were often selected to be trained on the job for more skilled positions, but women never were.

The foreman's reaction was typical. First, he smiled and tried to flirt away our seriousness. This was his standard way of dealing with individual complaints. It's the "nice guy" way of convincing other people that they really have no grievances. After all, who wants to be unpleasant and insistent and make a scene with such a friendly boss?

But he wasn't dealing with one lone woman. He saw we meant business. So he dropped the charm and told us solemnly that certainly he was very concerned about opportunities for women but it was up to the supervisors to decide who would be promoted and he couldn't discuss the matter with us.

When we answered that we were painfully aware that

the supervisors were in full control of promotions, but that we didn't like the way they decided things, he just shrugged. After an hour of going around in circles we told him we'd had enough for the time being and went back to work.

The foreman's reaction was no surprise. But what was a surprise was the reaction of the other women in the department when we got back.

They thought we were just out for ourselves. They thought we just wanted our friend to get a better job and to find out how we could get better jobs. They didn't see any point in supporting us just so we could cash in.

I was really surprised. I thought that even if women were afraid to support another woman publicly, they would identify with her.

But then I started to think: what was in it for them? Why should they care if one woman got a promotion? Why should they care if a woman was made supervisor over them instead of a man?

There were a few women in lower supervisory positions in the plant. (In 10 or 15 years they had advanced as far as men advanced in 1 or 2 years.) They were generally not trusted and not liked. It wasn't hard to see that they felt very shaky in their positions. They felt they had to do better than any man to keep their jobs. Better meant squeezing more work out of the rest of us.

A standard excuse for not promoting women to supervisory positions is that even women don't like women supervisors. People use a double standard. A man can be petty and mean and he's admired for being hard-driving. A woman can be conscientious and she's attacked for being bitchy.

But many women do bear down on the people under them. One of the older lead women took her friend aside and advised her that the only way to get ahead in the company was to not get close to any of the other women and to do whatever the male supervisors wanted.

So when women do become "bitchy" it's because they have learned that this is the only way they can succeed. They have to break off from other women workers to show the higher-ups they can be trusted.

And because everyone is just waiting for them to make one false move to say "I told you so — women can't do that job," they have to drive much harder than any man. If you beat a dog and then continually dangle a stick from your hand, he'll either turn mean or lose his spirit and crawl away.

So the women in my department were not looking forward to any more women supervisors.

How about the possibility of them getting promoted, with higher pay and more interesting work? What if we could force management to give women equal chances at promotion, like the men?

The women weren't impressed. They knew there wasn't much room at the top. (Even when the top is only $3.10 an hour.) The majority of women know that they aren't going to be the lucky one to get the job, no matter how hard they try.

So the whole issue of ending discrimination against women in promotions doesn't hold out much hope to the majority of women. Even if women were given equal consideration for promotions tomorrow, most women would still be stuck with the same problems.

What are those problems? What kind of work were women doing? What did they get out of it? What did they go home to after the work day was over?

In our department, as in every department, the work women were assigned to was brainless, boring work. Like drilling one hole in the same place on a metal bar, 2,000 to 3,000 times a day, day after day.

Often we worked with irritating chemicals that inflamed our hands and arms for weeks. One poorly ventilated room was filled with methyl benzene fumes (like the stuff in airplane glue) within a few minutes after work began.

I used to come to work feeling fine in the morning. Within an hour I would feel myself slowing down, my head getting tighter, and for the rest of the day I would be dizzy and in a daze.

At first I thought I was getting migraine headaches until I realized that this only happened in this one room. In this same room there was a machine that gave out very high frequency sounds. Beep beep beep all day long. We complained a little, but didn't push it, because the answer always was, "If you don't like it, leave."

Then the office workers upstairs complained, after they figured out where their headaches were coming from. So the machine was moved . . . to another place where it wouldn't bother the office workers, only more women production workers.

All this wasn't just something to put up with for 8 hours and then go home and leave all behind. I would go home totally wiped out from the combination of the fumes, the noise, and the numbing work. For several months I was good for nothing after work. Saturdays I'd sit around, letting my head clear. Sundays I'd finally have myself together enough to actually go out, visit friends, see a movie, etc. But on Monday it all caved in again. (And that's what it really felt like.)

But I didn't have it so bad. I was single, with no family responsibilities. So I could just go home and collapse, or lie around on weekends.

Most of the women were married or divorced with children. Their day started several hours before work, getting husbands and children ready for the day. After work, they would rush to get dinner and spend their evenings doing various household and family tasks.

They got little help from their husbands. "After all," a man needs to take it easy after a hard day at work. But how about a woman after an equally hard day at her job?

As for weekends, most of the women worked Saturdays when they could get the overtime. No one was working for pin money. At $2.00 to $2.70 an hour, you work overtime just to make ends meet. (With this pay rate, Omark was actually ahead of most factories in the area. Usually women are paid nothing more than minimum wage.)

One serious financial burden was the cost of child-care for pre-school children. This ran an average of $15 a week *per child:* $15 or $30 out of take-home pay of $60 to $85.

This is hardest for women with several children but no husband.

There was supposed to be one way women at Omark could get ahead. They couldn't work their way up directly through the company. But they could go to school and learn special skills and then apply for better jobs. The company even paid 80% of tuition and books for courses approved by the supervisor as being relevant to your job. This sounded like a good deal. But very few women could take advantage of it.

It's hard for anyone working full-time to go to school. But it's even harder for a married woman with children and household responsibilities. Besides, if you can barely afford day care while you work, you don't have enough to pay for even more babysitting while you go to night school.

With the higher wages men made (they started at the highest a woman could make, and they got raises every month for the first three, while we got them every other month) a single guy could save up enough in a couple of years to quit and go to school full-time for awhile.

But even a single woman barely made enough to support herself, much less save to go to school. So the "opportunity" wasn't within reach of most women.

One thing that the workers at Omark didn't know about was the large contributions men like John Gray, Chairman of the Omark Board of Directors, make to various colleges. Gray is also President of the Board of Trustees of Reed College, and Ross Thompson, Acting President of Reed, is another Omark director.

For several years Gray has made major contributions to Reed. He is only one example.

So it seemed like Omark was trying to help out its employees with picking up tuition and books tabs for part-time schooling. But at the same time a much larger chunk of Omark profits were being turned over to Reed and other schools, where middle-class and upper-middle-class students get full tuition, room and board scholarships.

No Omark employee could ever hope that she or any of

her children would ever make it into the big time, like Reed. So Omark really wasn't doing very much to help working people get ahead. "Liberal" and "progressive" company policies were a smokescreen for the bulk of activities that fed the status quo.

So this is what it's like for the many women in the Portland area that work in factories. An end to discrimination in promotions won't help them. An Equal Rights Amendment that takes away their coffee breaks and allows employers to work them overtime against their wishes and without overtime pay won't help them. Most of them aren't going to get anywhere trying *individually* to get somewhere. This only divides them and makes them jealous and suspicious of each other.

No Pride in This Dust

by Bennett Kremen

On a Greyhound speeding through a dark, icy night toward Chicago, I return to old memories of packing lunch bags and pulling on greasy overalls each morning before rushing desperately to beat the factory time clock — months and months of this drudgery my reward for temporarily dropping out of a Chicago high school during the mid-1950s. Now I head once more toward that muscular city on the lake, to struggle again with time clocks and lunch bags — this time driven not by necessity but curiosity.

Only seven others, mostly students picked up in a college town, share the heavy darkness inside the bus. And now, with recent memories of a tough month I've spent in Detroit futilely searching for work in the car plants, I can't help wondering about the boy nearby with the backpack, the long-haired one behind him, the shoeless girls in front of me. For though they're all dressed as insurgents in a rebellion against technology, they surely know little of the sooty bowels of industry, where millions their own age labor each day. Yet I quickly hear bitter voices behind me as we reach the flame-tinted skies over Gary:

"Wow — look at that mess!"

"Yeah, they're even burning up the clouds!"

"Why don't they just turn it all into a frisbee field?"

Laughter travels through the bus, and a flurry of conversation continues all the way into Chicago's Loop. And though I've heard similar exchanges countless times, I couldn't

Reprinted with permission of the author and *Dissent* Magazine. Copyright © 1972 by *Dissent*.

help being impressed again by such intense expressions of "alienation from the tools of production" by these fortunate people, even if it's only fashionable prattle. For they're the ones benefiting the most from industry and grunting the least in its service. What about those who grunt the most?

The sun isn't up yet and the "Hawk," Chicago's cruel wind, lashes down on the thousands of workers huddling at bus stops. Even in my heavy laborer's clothes, this frigid journey to the Southworks is an agony, for that mile-long mill owned by the United States Steel Corporation squats on the damp shore of Lake Michigan. But the final bitter reward for playing the early bird is having to queue up now in the frost outside the gate, waiting for the seven o'clock shift to start.

"That's when they open the employment office, isn't it?"

"Uh-huh."

The fellow I'm talking to has a huge, blond mustache and is wearing an army jacket with Vietnam markings on it; he seems as disgusted as I am.

"Been looking long?" I ask.

"Three months. But I think they're hiring here."

"They are," I assure him. "Maybe we'll get lucky."

"Lucky . . . ?" He shrugs and looks up at the rows of smoke stacks and blast furnaces, ". . . if you want to call it that."

When the gate finally opens, he rushes into the employment office like the rest of us and quickly fills out cards passed out by a guard. This haste, however, is only a wasted effort. The hours trickle away in this increasingly crowded room without a word said to most of us. All we can do is wait and stare.

All around me are young people, many fresh out of high school and the Army — or off the streets of the South Side. Most seem remarkably free of that classical, humble, hungry look of the job hunter. Throughout the morning they stream in like locusts. This isn't only the ordinary consequence of unemployment: crowded into this room are men who were conceived during the baby boom in the 1940s and '50s, now hitting industry as once the country's school systems. And this pounding on the doors can only intensify as the average age of workers in mills and factories continues to tumble dramatically year by year — as it has since 1968. By the end of the decade, 68 percent of the labor force will be below thirty-four, a sharp reversal of the age distributions during the '50s and early '60s. Already men in their twenties constitute a third of organized labor's entire membership.

As I look around, unpredictable things are confronting me. Where are the Polish kids who traditionally flock to this mill? For decades legend has always designated the Southworks, the huge mills next door in East Chicago, and the industrial wilds of Gary below it as a land flowing with *kolbassi* and boilermakers. Yet 70 percent of those here are black — yes, young, black, and beautiful. For they aren't wearing the overalls, that drab, humble uniform of the working stiff: their "vines," man, are their own — purple silk shirts with collars hanging halfway to their waists, fur coats, four-cornered velvet hats, and bright, multicolored shoes that mock this somber environment where roughly 9.5 percent of all U.S. Steel's raw tonnage is poured. Watching these men filing one by one into the interviewing section, their loose ghetto walk declaring the assertiveness of the mean streets of the city, makes me wonder if the steel industry has produced a *confidential* document similar to the gloomy one put out in Detroit in 1969 by Malcolm Denise, Ford Motor Company's top labor-relations man.

"More than 35 percent of [Ford's 1968 work force] . . . ," he confided at a company management conference, "were nonwhite, compared to 15 percent in 1960." Then, after predicting unique labor troubles because of that anticipated flood of young workers into industry, he concluded with this warning: "Another feature of the landscape in which we will be operating [in the '70s] is our increasing dependence on blacks to get our work done. Whatever some may feel about the black issue in general, we are in fact dependent, and will continue to be, on black people to make this company go."

"Hey," I whisper to the fellow next to me with the big,

blond mustache, "are there always so many spades looking for jobs around here?"

"Sure."

"What about in East Chicago?"

"Oh, those dudes are workin' all down the lake, even past Gary."

"What's happened to the Polish people who used to work these places?"

"They're still around — the older ones mostly. A lot of 'em moved away though and never want to come back around here anymore."

"Will working with all these black guys bother you?" I inquire suddenly. For a moment he eyes me warily before responding:

"Will it bother you, man?"

"No."

"Well, I don't give a damn either."

We keep on talking, trying to beat the boredom of this incessant waiting. He tells me that even the local union president at the Southworks is a black man. Since this local is a large one in one of the largest steel-producing regions in the country, that's probably quite important, I tell him. Well, not only Local 65 but the whole region, he figures, will probably be mostly black in ten years.

"Then for the first time, we'll see *black power* with real muscle behind it," I tell him. "And even if the blacks here don't really know it yet, that power probably already exists."

A sudden thoughtfulness — or is it distress — hovers in my young friend's eyes. And quickly I shift away from talk about race, even though he seems too indifferent to really care about it either way — and though that very indifference, if real, intrigues me. For such a sentiment would be a striking departure from the monolithic hatreds that flourished among the men I worked with in this city less than 15 years ago. These questions must remain hanging, for I'm being called for an interview.

Early the next morning, I'm in a room again with about 20 others — most of them young, many of them black — listening to a black personnel man in expensive tweeds playing the lay-it-on-the-line role:

"What I'm telling you now is the same for blacks and whites — there ain't no difference, because at least five of you, that's 25 percent," he says, "won't even last out the six-week probationary period — blacks or whites. But jobs are tight, so more of you might stick it out this year than last. Listen, I ain't going to lie to you — some of those foremen are nothin' but bigots, and I know that. But you don't settle things by hittin' 'em up side the head. And listen," he says with sudden urgency, "you just gotta come in every day; you just gotta come in on time!" And though he speaks now about not keeping valuables in our lockers 'cause dudes searching for marijuana or money will wrench them right open, he expresses far more concern in another plea for us "to get in here every day. If you can't make it, you gotta at least call in and let them know. Man, I don't know why guys don't even call in."

Though this lecture is inappropriate for the beefy, red-headed fellow next to me droning on about fringe benefits and buying a house with a paneled basement, I'm sure that the man in front of us isn't simply wasting his breath on ominous predictions. And as we're being loaded now into a bus to be taken to our assigned locations, I'm almost convinced that what I'm about to experience might have little resemblance to my working days of — well — *long ago*.

Yet some things are ageless, like this ride through the teeming, fenced-in mill past flatcars loaded down with huge, glowing ingots of raw steel that cast their heat like giant radiators. We bump along past dozens of roads, ore docks, rail lines, and shops, some a block long and hissing and clanging with the sounds of hammers, alarm bells, and deadly molten metal that rears from the furnaces like harsh sunshine. Awe — and a touch of uneasiness — shows on the young faces of those sharing the bus with me, their feelings surely paralleling my own. For to the uninitiated, it seems impossible that all these steaming slag piles and ore boats, blast furnaces and cranes that travel on tracks far above us can be managed by 8,200 mere workers, though they labor around the clock in three swing shifts every day of the year.

"If they ain't got a lot of machines to do all this goddamn work," I announce in a fool-around tone, "we're all gonna have a sore back!"

"I'm hip — better they use a dynamo than Little Joe. They ain't got no spare parts for me, man!"

The laughter is heavy, though only the driver and a few new workers are left in the bus — Little Joe among them. And now, smack on the shore of the lake, where the wind hits like a razor, the driver calls out his last stop — our stop.

"This is #2 Electric Furnace — only a half-hour walking time to the gate."

He is smiling when he says it, but none of us stepping out into the damp cold share his amusement.

"You gotta be jivin' man — you mean from now on we gotta hoof it!"

"That's it, Little Joe — coming in and going out."

A low, angry grumbling at the thought of this cold, pay-less walk each day fades only gradually as we follow the driver through this noisy, dirty building to the foreman's office. When we enter, the grumbling is over, but a sullen silence remains.

"OK — each of you have a number on the card they gave you. Memorize it, because that's what you're going to be called around here."

31-445, then, is who I am to the pair of foremen in blue hard hats who've just given each of us a bright yellow helmet worn by production workers on labor gangs. For $3.19 an hour then, with a bit extra for late shifts and weekends, we now conclude these sterile preliminaries and don our hard hats, joining tens of thousands of other young workers thus initiated into the lowest ranks of the steel industry.

"Some of you young guys take too many days off! I just don't stand for that shit, or for you comin' in late either!" The sudden tough talk comes from Stanley, the smaller of the two foremen whose unpronounceable Polish last name is tagged to his helmet. The taller one, Mr. Lis, continues now, but in a gentler voice:

"Yeah fellows — you won't get ahead, you know, if you

do this AWOL stuff. And we want you to get ahead. So you try to watch those absences, huh?"

Neither this easy sell nor the shock tactics seem to ruffle the skepticism of my fellow workers, for they must have sensed, as I did, that Lis and Stanley were only going through a feeble ritual that neither of them really believed would prove effective. Behind Stanley's bluster and Lis's "sincerity" was a note almost of despair.

Had the foremen I'd once worked for displayed such helplessness, I would've been startled. But I'd already heard young workers in Detroit barrooms and bowling alleys groaning about having to face another day of tedium on the assembly line and boasting about how often they'd gone AWOL.

"Our generation hated that line too," a clever old workingman told me in a bar off Cadillac Square, "but you had a lot of guys proud to work for them big companies in those days. Remember that type? These kids have a different outlook on life. They've never been broke the way we were, and they've got a hell-of-a-lot more schoolin'. You want to know somethin' — *they don't even know how to take the crap we took!*"

Though he didn't speak of affluence and alienation, of levels of aspiration and the breakdown of traditional motivations, that old-timer summarized much of what I'd heard for almost a month from union officials, economists, and worried business executives all over Detroit: a mood of quiet despair descends in those executive offices when they lay out the statistics on their absenteeism problem and speculate on its long-range effects.

"From 1957 to '61," I was told at Ford, "we averaged 2.6 percent of our production workers off on a given day. Each year since then, the figure rose until it reached 5.8 percent in 1968. On Mondays and Fridays, though, the figure often goes almost to 15 percent. And that really hurts inside those plants. Right now we're averaging 5.1 percent for the year."

"You mean you're still averaging that high even after three years of recession and inflation?"

"Yes."

"Then you're going to need chronic economic trouble to cut that figure — a catastrophe."

"I guess so — but believe me, nobody's praying for it!"

At General Motors I was told by a major official that productivity and the quality of cars coming off the line are affected adversely by absenteeism — and that it enhances inflation. "This is a serious matter, and we certainly talked about it quite a bit with the union during the 1970 negotiations. These absences are occurring in every geographical area — and all races and types of people are involved." Though only 15 percent of the work force at GM generates most of the late arrivals and absences, he went on, most of these men are concentrated among the newer workers under 35. "They often take one or even two days off every week." When I asked him what he thought the outcome will be if this continues, I was given a brief lecture on the fall of Rome. Although this sort of instant Latin scholarship usually makes me impatient, I was impressed by his calm pessimism; for it was dramatic as perhaps only an immensely powerful man's pessimism can be when an element of habitual control is suddenly defying his grasp.

"It happened in the schools; it's happening in the Army —" Louie Streho, an old salt running the Detroit branch of the seamen's union, told me. "Why the hell did they ever think it wouldn't happen in the factories!"

In the mill now, as I lean leisurely on one of the brooms Stanley had thrust upon us, I begin to wonder about all this unexpected time I seem to have just to muse about things like Louie's bit of wisdom. I soon find out, from a few old mill hands, that these brooms we're pushing around often just keep us busy until enough men are AWOL — and we're really needed. . . .

Yanagan leads me through a dark corner of the shop now, his eyes cast cautiously at the overhead cranes scooping up scrap for the insatiable furnaces upstairs.

"Psssst! ! Hey!"

Hissing at us from behind a half-filled gondola car is Tommy Thumbs, and huddled uncommonly close to him are

Little Joe, two vets recently back from Vietnam, and the new Italian kid.

"It's a downer day, man — let's lift it up!" Tommy passes a joint to Yanagan who draws the smoke deep, then hands it to me. For a moment I hesitate till Little Joe pats me on the shoulder and says: "What you waiting for? When you're feeling bad, you take medicine, right? Well, this place makes ye feel sick, and you got the medicine right in your hand!"

The smoke striking into my lungs sends my blood leaping. And soon the flying sparks, the hot steel, the raging, exploding furnaces above us seem like frivolities on a carnival night. . . .

Not all the mills in the country are quite like this one, I'm told. But old hands insist they will be, as the older workers retire in the next five years.

"Maybe some big doses of economic trouble will shape these kids up," a tough-minded company man told me in Pittsburgh. "But that's liable to murder us too. And I'd hate to see too many of this breed out on the streets without jobs. I just don't think it'd be healthy." Others both in Pittsburgh and Detroit reminded me that plenty of the younger workers — indeed many I've met — are diligently paying off mortgages and working hard for a second car, "and when that other type gets older and has a few kids, everything'll probably settle down." Yet when I asked what'll happen until then, I got only a shrug of the shoulders. A few clever economists, however, point out that the steel industry has invested more than $10 billion in capital expenditures since 1965, but that the expected soaring increases in productivity associated with such a huge investment hasn't materialized. The "productivity puzzle" is what this unprecedented mystery, found not only in the steel industry, is being called. And it's haunting the financial wizards of Wall Street and Washington. I recommend they spend a few days in a labor shack getting it all straight.

"Tommy — you've been out for two days. Don't you miss the bread?"

"I can get by. I rather have the time than the money."

"You know — if jobs stay tight, the company'll probably start cracking down hard."

A sudden, angry silence falls, and all the men in the shack are staring at me. But I keep on talking because after four weeks of digging choking lime from degasser pits, hooking scrap to cranes, and sweeping miles of dust and grime into neat little piles the way they do, I'm entitled to their trust. "What if they crack down, Yanni?"

"They don't own me, man! If I want a day off, I take a day off. Nothin's gonna stop that!"

"What if they fire you?"

"Then let 'em fire me. I ain't seen 'em do it yet."

"Why not?"

" 'Cause the next guy who comes along is going to do the same thing I am."

Not all these young men are so bitter, and some even work hard — when they show up. But neither whites, blacks, skilled workers, laborers, militants nor conservatives — and there are conservatives — are thankful to the company for providing them with jobs.

"Oh — that's strictly Mickey Mouse," a young Polish millwright with hair flowing from under his hard hat said to me. "You find some guys upstairs talking that way — but not many my age. This company is using me to make money: I use them the same way. And that's all. . . ."

Another skilled worker, this one with short hair, who averages at least $5 an hour and who moonlights as a cop in the suburbs where he lives, told me: "The job's not bad, but this company stinks. You don't get anything from them without a fight."

"What about the union?"

"You got to keep on their ass too."

"Any niggers working in your unit?"

"A few."

"Don't they bother you?"

"No — why should they?"

"Plenty of the older guys can't stand them."

"Some of the younger guys can't stand them either — but I don't think we're so steamed up about them. I'll tell you something, a lot of those black guys won't take any crap from the company. I don't mind working with them at all."

A few weeks later Ed Hojnachi, the treasurer at Local 65 of the Steelworkers union, my local, told me that he first realized things were profoundly changing when Bob Hatch, a black man, was elected president of 65. I answered that I wasn't at all surprised this had happened, "not after what I've been hearing in the mill. And you know, Ed, a lot of locals in the Auto Workers have been taken by blacks too — with strong support from some young white workers."

"Well, it's about time. I guess they want a fighter these days — whoever he is."

"Yes — and maybe it's about time," I hear echoed from Ed Sadlowski, who nine years ago, in an era when local union power simply wasn't challenged, took the presidency of 65. He was only 23 then: today he's Bob Hatch's strongest supporter and, at 32, has his eye on the leadership of the entire Chicago-Gary-Milwaukee-Joliet district — a crucial one in the 1.2 million-man United Steelworkers of America.

"Of course there are changes coming," he says as he tours me now through the Bush, the neighborhood around the mill where the skies blaze every night and the barrooms are seldom empty. "In 1965 — get this! — only a few hundred disciplines were issued to the guys in the Southworks. Guess how many the company gave out last year?" The number must have leaped, I was sure, but to hear just how much stuns me: "... that's right, 3,400 disciplines in 1970 — for coming late, for not coming at all, for swearing, arguing, drinking. And the company guys are moaning. They'd love the union to play copper and get everyone in on time for 'em — sure!"

"What do you tell them?"

"No sir — that's not my job. 'Make life better in those mills!' That's what I tell them."

Eddie takes me for a shot and a beer to a bar with music from Durango or Huahuaca blaring from its juke box, an establishment run by a brother of his friend and colleague from Local 65, Johnny Chico; then through the black section of the Bush where exhausted frame houses hug the edge of the Southworks; and finally to Marti and Joe's at the mill gate where, this time, polkas from Cracow or Warsaw blast from the juke box.

Men fresh off the second shift with mill dust still in their throats eagerly belly up to the bar. Its blunt, plain mahogany and the heavy laughter of the men leaning against it would be home to John Garfield — except for the TV flashing images from outer space and the long-haired young worker next to us in the red-white-and-blue cleatless track shoes.

Soon Eddie begins talking to him and his drinking partner who works in the same shop. He asks why they don't come to union meetings, and they tell him that they're boring. He asks if they'd like to see things changing in the mill. They would. He asks if a lot of other young workers feel that way too. Many do. Then what can be done to make those changes come about? Their answer is a feeble shrug.

"Listen," he says, "you got to give more if you want more. I don't mean just wanting cash — I mean a better life. The union has to give more too. Sure, bread and butter's important — but maybe we spend too much time just thinking about money. Those companies (if they know what's good for them) and the unions too — everybody should be thinking, and soon, about giving people better lives."

Snow is blowing in through the open doors of the shop and steam rising from a slag pile by the lake turns suddenly eerie as the late-shift moon breaks through the clouds. The month is coming to an end, and so are my last hours in the mill. Despite the ceaseless clanging of metal echoing through the shop, the early morning brings a rare calm.

"Say José — did they really used to fire you after only three disciplines?" I'm talking to an intense, talkative old laborer who'd been in the mill more than 25 years.

"Sure they did. Now some of these young kids got six, seven, even eight of 'em and they're still around."

"How does that make you older workers feel?"

"We laugh."

"No kidding!"

"Sure — 'cause those foremen used to be so tough. You'd

stop shovelin' for a few minutes and they'd say, 'What's the matter, you tired?' Now they catch these kids sleepin' on a bench and they don't even say nothin'. We're laughin' all right."

"But aren't you mad at the kids too?"

"Sometimes, especially when you gotta carry the load for 'em. But I'll tell you, they've made gentlemen out of a lot of those company guys — not the big shots, I mean the company guys right here in the plants."

"What's going to happen after you older fellows retire, and it's only younger workers in here?"

"I don't know — sometimes we wonder if there's gonna be a mill anymore. One thing's sure — it ain't gonna be the way it used to be!"

The sun is finally rising over the lake now, and tired men with dirt-streaked faces begin trudging into the locker room. After good-byes to José, I join the others at the huge wash basins and, imitating those around me, fiercely scrub the mill from my skin like a guilty man. How determined Yanagan, Tommy Thumbs, Charlie Chan, and even José are with that soap and water, for there's no pride in this dust, nor joy in the frigid walk along the lake to the gate where we hand in our cards to a guard and pass into the outside world.

"Hey," I say to Tommy Thumbs while we're standing in the street waiting for a bus, "should they turn this whole damn mill into a frisbee field?"

"Into what, man?"

"Forget it, Tommy — it's just a stupid idea."

PART TWO

Appraising the New Mood

The Change in Attitudes Toward Work

from *Work in America*

Although social scientists have long disputed the precise contribution of the Protestant ethic to the genesis of capitalism, they generally agree that thrift, hard work, and a capacity for deferring gratification historically were traits widely distributed among Americans. Moreover, as part of the legitimacy of the economic system, individual members of our society were to be credited or blamed for their own circumstances, according to the degree of their prosperity.

But the ethic, or what has passed for it, appears to be under attack. Some futurists tell us that automation will make work unnecessary for most people, and that we may as well ignore work and look to other matters, such as "creative leisure." More immediately, our attention is drawn to these alleged signs of work's obsolescence:

— The growth in the number of communes
— Numerous adolescents panhandling in such meccas as Georgetown, North Beach, and the Sunset Strip
— Various enterprises shifting to 4-day workweeks
— Welfare caseloads increasing
— Retirement occurring at ever earlier ages.

All of these are relatively benign signs; more malignant signs are found in reduced productivity and in the doubling of man-days per year lost from work through strikes. In some industries there apparently is a rise in absenteeism, sabotage, and turnover rates.

Ironically, many of these symptoms have increased despite the general improvements in physical conditions and mone-

Reprinted from *Work in America*, Report of a Special Task Force to the Secretary of Health, Education, and Welfare; The MIT Press, 1973.

tary rewards for work. In comparison with the dreary lot of most workers during the industrial revolution and, indeed, until quite recently, the workplace today is an Elysian field. Sweatshop conditions have all but disappeared. The extreme dangers of work appear to have declined in most industries. Women and children are seldom engaged in back-breaking drudgery. Arbitrary wage cuts and dismissals are relatively rare, and enlightened laws, personnel policies, and labor unions protect the worker in a variety of ways.

Quantitatively, the lives of workers away from work similarly have improved. Real income, standard of living, health status, and life expectancy have all risen markedly. Among most classes of workers, homes and cars are owned in abundance, and bank accounts continually grow. For those without work, there is social security, unemployment compensation, workman's compensation, and an income floor will very likely be established under welfare compensation. On the average, then, no workers have ever been as materially well-off as American workers are today. What, then, is wrong?

Social scientists are suggesting that the root of the problem is to be found in the changing needs, aspirations, and values of workers. For example, Abraham Maslow has suggested that the needs of human beings are hierarchical and, as each level is filled, the subsequent level becomes salient. This order of needs is:

1. Physiological requirements (food, habitat, etc.)
2. Safety and security
3. Companionship and affection
4. Self-esteem and the esteem of others
5. Self-actualization (being able to realize one's potential to the full).

It may be argued that the very success of industry and organized labor in meeting the basic needs of workers has unintentionally spurred demands for esteemable and fulfilling jobs.

Frederick Herzberg suggests an alternative way of looking at the needs of workers — in terms of intrinsic and extrinsic factors. Under this rubric, job satisfaction and dissatisfaction are not opposites but two separate dimensions. Extrinsic factors, such as inadequate pay, incompetent supervision, or dirty working conditions may lead to dissatisfaction, which may be reduced in turn by such "hygienic" measures as higher pay and "human relations" training for foremen. But such actions will not make workers satisfied. Satisfaction depends on the provision of intrinsic factors, such as achievement, accomplishment, responsibility, and challenging work. Satisfaction, then, is a function of the content of work; dissatisfaction, of the environment of work. Increases in productivity have been found to correlate in certain industries and occupations with increases in satisfaction, but not with decreases in dissatisfaction. Hence, hygienic improvements may make work tolerable, but will not necessarily raise motivation or productivity. The latter depends on making jobs more interesting and important.

A recent survey, which lends some support for this emphasis on job content, was undertaken by the Survey Research Center, University of Michigan, with support from the Department of Labor. This unique and monumental study is based on a representative sample of 1,533 American workers at all occupational levels. When these workers were asked how important they regarded some 25 aspects of work, they ranked in order of importance:

1. Interesting work
2. Enough help and equipment to get the job done
3. Enough information to get the job done
4. Enough authority to get the job done
5. Good pay
6. Opportunity to develop special abilities
7. Job security
8. Seeing the results of one's work.

What the workers want most, as more than 100 studies in the past 20 years show, is to become masters of their immediate environments and to feel that their work and they themselves are important — the twin ingredients of self-esteem. Workers recognize that some of the dirty jobs can be transformed only into the merely tolerable, but the most oppressive features of work are felt to be avoidable: constant supervision and coercion, lack of variety, monotony, meaningless tasks, and isolation. An increasing number of workers want more autonomy in tackling their tasks, greater opportunity for increasing their skills, rewards that are directly connected to the intrinsic aspects of work, and greater participation in the design of work and the formulation of their tasks.

When we cite the growing problem in the country of job dissatisfaction using the criteria laid out above, are we talking about 5% or 50% of the workers in the country? It is clear that classically alienating jobs (such as on the assembly line) that allow the worker no control over the conditions of work and that seriously affect his mental and physical functioning off the job probably comprise less than 2% of the jobs in America. But a growing number of white-collar jobs have much in common with the jobs of autoworkers and steelworkers. Indeed, discontent with the intrinsic factors of work has spread even to those with managerial status. It is, however, almost as difficult to measure these feelings of discontent about work as it is to measure such other basic feelings as pride, love, or hate. Most of the leading experts on work in America have expressed disappointment over the unsophisticated techniques commonly used to measure work dissatisfaction.

The Gallup poll, for example, asks only "Is your work satisfying?" It is not surprising that they get from 80% to 90% positive responses (but even this crude measure shows a steady decrease in satisfaction over the last decade). When a similar question was asked of auto and assembly-line workers, 60% reported that their jobs were "interesting." Does this mean that such high percentages of blue-collar workers *are really satisfied* with their jobs? Most researchers say no. Since a substantial portion of blue-collar workers (1) report being satisfied with their jobs *but also indicate they wish to change them* and (2) report they would continue working even if they didn't have to *but only to fill time,* then this can only mean that these workers accept the necessity of work but expect little satisfaction from their specific jobs.

Those workers who report that they are "satisfied" are

really saying that they are not "dissatisfied" in Herzbergian terms — i.e., their pay and security are satisfactory, but this does not necessarily mean that their work is intrinsically rewarding. This distinction is illustrated by an interview sociologist George Strauss held with a blue-collar worker on a routine job. This worker told Strauss, in a rather offhand way, "I got a pretty good job." "What makes it such a good job?" Strauss responded. The worker answered:

> Don't get me wrong. I didn't say it is a *good* job. It's an O.K. job—about as good a job as a guy like me might expect. The foreman leaves me alone and it pays well. But I would never call it a good job. It doesn't amount to much, but it's not bad.

Robert Kahn suggests that the direct question of satisfaction strikes too closely to one's self-esteem to be answered simply:

> For most workers it is a choice between no work connection (usually with severe attendant economic penalties and a conspicuous lack of meaningful alternative activities) and a work connection which is burdened with negative qualities (routine, compulsory scheduling, dependency, etc.). In these circumstances, the individual has no difficulty with the choice; he chooses work, pronounces himself moderately satisfied, and tells us more only if the questions become more searching. Then we learn that he can order jobs clearly in terms of their status or desirability, wants his son to be employed differently from himself, and, if given a choice, would seek a different occupation.

More sophisticated measures of job satisfaction designed to probe the specific components of a job offer great contradictions to simple "Are you satisfied?" surveys. When it asked about specific working conditions, the Michigan survey found that great numbers of "satisfied" workers had major dissatisfactions with such factors as the quality of supervision and the chance to grow on a job. A 1970-71 survey of white, male, blue-collar workers found that less than one-half claimed that they were satisfied with their jobs most of the time. The proportion of positive responses varied according to the amount of variety, autonomy, and meaningful responsibility their jobs provided.

Over the last two decades, one of the most reliable single indicators of job dissatisfaction has been the response to the question: "What type of work would you try to get into if you could start all over again?" Most significantly, of a cross section of white-collar workers (including professionals), only 43% would voluntarily choose the same work that they were doing, and only 24% of a cross section of blue-collar workers would choose the same kind of work if given another chance (see Table below). This question, some researchers feel, is

Table: Percentages in Occupational Groups Who Would Choose Similar Work Again

Professional and Lower White-Collar Occupations	%	Working-Class Occupations	%
Urban university professors	93	Skilled printers	52
Mathematicians	91	Paper workers	42
Physicists	89	Skilled autoworkers	41
Biologists	89	Skilled steelworkers	41
Chemists	86	Textile workers	31
Firm lawyers	85	*Blue-collar workers, cross section*	*24*
Lawyers	83	Unskilled steelworkers	21
Journalists (Washington correspondents)	82	Unskilled autoworkers	16
Church university professors	77		
Solo lawyers	75		
White-collar workers, cross section	*43*		

a particularly sensitive indicator because it causes respondents to take into account the intrinsic factors of the job and the very personal question of self-esteem. Those in jobs found to be least satisfying on other measures seldom would choose their present occupation again.

Another fairly accurate measure of job satisfaction is to ask the worker the question: "What would you do with the extra two hours if you had a 26-hour day?" Two out of three college professors and one out of four lawyers say they would use the extra time in a work-related activity. Strikingly, only one out of twenty nonprofessional workers would make use of the extra time in work activity.

We are able, then, to differentiate between those jobs that are satisfying and those that are dissatisfying to the people who hold them. The prestige of an occupation is often an accurate predictor of the level of satisfaction found in a job (while the ranking of occupations by prestige does not correspond exactly with either salary or the amount of education needed to perform well on the job). Moreover, prestige ranking of jobs is nearly identical with the ranking of jobs according to who would choose the same work again. Evidently, people know what work is satisfying and what work is not, even if they are unable to articulate the characteristics of each.

We also find that the jobs people find most satisfying contain most or all of the factors cited previously that workers find important in their jobs. The dissatisfying jobs contain only some or none of these factors. (Those jobs with highly dissatisfying aspects are found to correlate with social problems such as physical and mental illness.)

Demographic factors also play a part in the difference between satisfaction and dissatisfaction in the workplace. Young workers and blacks were found to be the most dissatisfied segments of the population in the University of Michigan Survey of Working Conditions. But even dissatisfaction among these groups was often found to correlate with specific kinds of jobs and job situations. For example, highly trained women in low-level jobs were often extremely dissatisfied, but women and men with the same training in the same jobs were equally satisfied.

SOURCES OF DISSATISFACTION

Based on what we know about the attitudes of workers toward their jobs, we can identify the following two factors as being major sources of job dissatisfaction: the anachronism of Taylorism and diminishing opportunities to be one's own boss.

The Anachronism of Taylorism. Frederick Winslow Taylor, father of time and motion studies and author of *Principles of Scientific Management,* propagated a view of efficiency which, until recently, was markedly successful — so long as "success" was measured in terms of unit costs and output. Under his tutelage, work tasks were greatly simplified, fragmented, compartmentalized, and placed under continuous supervision. The worker's rewards depended on doing as he was told and increasing his output. Taylor's advice resulted in major, sometimes spectacular, increases in productivity.

Several events have occurred to make Taylorism anachronistic. Primarily, the workforce has changed considerably since his principles were instituted in the first quarter of this century. From a workforce with an average educational attainment of less than junior high school, containing a large contingent of immigrants of rural and peasant origin and resigned to cyclical unemployment, the workforce is now largely native-born, with more than a high school education on the average, and affluence-minded. And, traditional values that depended on authoritarian assertion alone for their survival have been challenged.

Simplified tasks for those who are not simple-minded, close supervision by those whose legitimacy rests only on a hierarchical structure, and jobs that have nothing but money to offer in an affluent age are simply rejected. For many of the new workers, the monotony of work and scale of organization and their inability to control the pace and style of work are cause for a resentment which they, unlike older workers, do not repress.

Attempts to reduce the harmful effects of Taylorism over the last two generations have not got at the nub of the problem. For example, the "human relations" school attempts to offset Taylor's primacy of the machine with "tender, loving care" for workers. This school (which has many adherents in personnel offices today) ignores the technological and production factors involved in a business. This approach concentrates on the enterprise as a social system — the workers are to be treated better, but their jobs remain the same. Neither the satisfaction of workers nor their productivity is likely to improve greatly from the human relations approach. Alternatives to Taylorism, therefore, must arise from the assumption that it is insufficient to adjust either people to technology or technology to people. It is necessary to consider both the social needs of the workers and the task to be performed. This viewpoint challenges much of what passes as efficiency in our industrial society.

Many industrial engineers feel that gains in productivity will come about mainly through the introduction of new technology. They feel that tapping the latent productivity of workers is a relatively unimportant part of the whole question of productivity. This is the attitude that was behind the construction of the General Motors auto plant in Lordstown, Ohio, the newest and most "efficient" auto plant in America. Early in 1972, workers there went out on strike over the pace of the line and the robot-like tasks that they were asked to perform. This event highlights the role of the human element in productivity: What does the employer gain by having a "perfectly efficient" assembly line if his workers are out on strike because of the oppressive and dehumanized experience of working on the "perfect" line? As the costs of absenteeism, wildcat strikes, turnover, and industrial sabotage become an increasingly significant part of the cost of doing business, it is becoming clear that the current concept of industrial efficiency conveniently but mistakenly ignores the social half of the equation.

It should be noted that Taylorism and a misplaced conception of efficiency is not restricted to assembly-lines or, for that matter, to the manufacturing sector of the economy. The service sector is not exempt. For example, in the medical care industry, the phenomenal growth in employment over the past decade or so has occurred largely in lower-level occupations. This growth has been accompanied by an attempt to increase the efficiency of the upper-level occupations through the delegation of tasks down the ladder of skills. This undoubtedly results in a greater efficiency in the utilization of manpower, but it rigidifies tasks, reduces the range of skills utilized by most of the occupations, increases routinization, and opens the door to job dissatisfaction for a new generation of highly educated workers.

As we have seen, satisfying jobs are most often those that incorporate factors found in high-status jobs — autonomy, working on a "whole" problem, participation in decision making. But as Ivar Berg and others have noted, as a result of countless public and private policies and decisions that determine our occupational structure, growth in occupational opportunities has occurred largely in middle and lower levels. The automation revolution that was to increase the demand for skilled workers (while decreasing the need for humans to do the worst jobs of society) has not occurred. What we *have* been able to do is to create such jobs as teacher aides, medical technicians, and computer keypunch operators — not jobs with "professional" characteristics. Undoubtedly, these jobs have opened opportunities for many who would otherwise have had no chance to advance beyond much lower-skilled positions. But it is illusory to believe that technology is opening new high-level jobs that are replacing low-level jobs. Most new jobs offer little in the way of "career" mobility — lab technicians do not advance along a path and become doctors.

This problem of a fairly static occupational structure presents society with a formidable barrier to providing greater job satisfaction to those below the pinnacle of the job pyramid. Without a technological revolution there is little hope of flattening out this structure in order to give more workers higher-status jobs. It then becomes crucial to infuse middle- and lower-level jobs with professional characteristics, particularly if we plan to continue offering higher and higher degrees of education to young people on the assumption that their increased expectations can be met by the world of work.

Diminishing Opportunities to Be One's Own Boss. Our economic, political, and cultural system has fostered the notion of independence and antonomy, a part of which is the belief that a hardworking person, even if he has little capital, can always make a go of it in business for himself. Or, to put it another way, if things get too bad in a dependent work situation, it has been felt that the individual could always strike out on his own.

This element of the American Dream is rapidly becoming myth, and disappearing with it is the possibility of realizing the character traits of independence and autonomy by going into business for oneself. The trend of the past 70 years or more, and particularly in recent years, has been a decrease in small independent enterprises and self-employment, and an increase in the domination of large corporations and government in the workforce. In the middle of the 19th century, less than half of all employed people were wage and salary workers. By 1950 it was 80%, and by 1970, 90%. Self-employed persons dropped from 18% in 1950 to 9% in 1970. Individual proprietorships in service trades declined from 81% to 78% in only five years — from 1958 to 1963. From 1960 to 1970, government workers increased from 12% of the civilian labor force to more than 15%. Out of 3,534,000 industrial units employing 70% of the civilian labor force, 2% of the units accounted for 50.6% of the employees, and more than 27% of the employed were accounted for in 0.3% of the units.

Among a class of occupations notable for their autonomy — managers, officials, and proprietors (excluding farms) — — self-employment fell from 50% in 1950 to 37% in 1960. On the farms, wage and salary workers increased as a percentage of all farm workers from 61% in 1950 to 80% in 1960. Even among authors, self-employment dropped from 62% to 38% in this period, while self-employed photographers declined from 41% to 34%. Although the percentage of self-employed lawyers has remained almost constant, in 1967 nearly half reported working in firms having 8 to 50 or more lawyers, suggesting some limitation on their autonomy and independence.

As these data attest, the trend is toward large corporations and bureaucracies which typically organize work in such a way as to minimize the independence of the workers and maximize control and predictability for the organization. Characterologically, the hierarchical organization requires workers to follow orders, which calls for submissive traits, while the selection of managers calls for authoritarian and controlling traits. With the shift from manufacturing to services — employment has gone from about 50-50 in 1950 to 62-38 in favor of services in 1970 — the tyranny of the machine is perhaps being replaced by the tyranny of the bureaucracy.

Yet, the more democratic and self-affirmative an individual is, the less he will stand for boring, dehumanized, and authoritarian work. Under such conditions, the workers either protest or give in, at some cost to their psychological well-being. Anger that does not erupt may be frozen into schizoid depressed characters who escape into general alienation, drugs, and fantasies. More typically, dissatisfying working environments result in the condition known as alienation.

> Alienation exists when workers are unable to control their immediate work processes, to develop a sense of purpose and function which connects their jobs to the over-all organization of production, to belong to integrated industrial communities, and when they fail to become involved in the activity of work as a mode of personal self-expression. (Robert Blauner, *Alienation and Freedom*)

Social scientists identify four ingredients of alienation: (1) powerlessness (regarding ownership of the enterprise, general management policies, employment conditions and the immediate work process), (2) meaninglessness (with respect to the character of the product worked on as well as the scope of the product or the production process), (3) isolation (the social aspect of work), and (4) self-estrangement ("depersonalized detachment," including boredom, which can lead to "absence of personal growth"). As thus broken down, alienation is inherent in pyramidal, bureaucratic management patterns and in advanced, Taylorized technology, which divides and subdivides work into minute, monotonous elements. The result of alienation is often the withdrawal of the worker from community or political activity or the displacement of his frustrations through participation in radical social or political movements.

It seems fair to conclude that the combination of the changing social character of American workers, declining opportunities to establish independence through self-employment, and an anachronistic organization of work can create an explosive and pathogenic mix.

Blue-Collar Blues on the Assembly Line

by Judson Gooding

I Spend 40 Hours a Week Here
— Am I Supposed to Work Too?

Sign in tavern near Ford Dearborn plant

Detroit knows a lot about building new cars, but there's a lot it doesn't know about the new young men building them. This failure to understand the men who do the work has meant, increasingly, failure to get the work done with maximum efficiency. The problem is particularly serious because the understanding gap, curiously reminiscent of the gaps between parents and children and between universities and students, faces off the nation's biggest industry against a very substantial percentage of its workers. There is labor unrest on many fronts, but nowhere else do venerable production techniques and a fractious new work force collide quite so dramatically. . . .

Of the 740,000 hourly paid workers building cars today, 40 percent are under thirty-five. The automobile industry, justly proud of its extraordinary record of past accomplishments, is totally committed to the assembly line which comes down from that past, and its heroes are veteran production men who know how to "move the iron." At the plant level, managers are trying to build cars by the old methods with new workers they don't understand and often don't much like. While at headquarters top executives are beginning to worry about "who's down there" on those assembly lines, what "they" are like, what "they" want from their jobs, there

Reprinted with permission of the author from *Fortune.* Copyright © 1970 by Judson Gooding.

is still a comprehension gap. This gap would be dangerous at any time, but it is particularly so in a grim sales year, a period of intensifying foreign competition, and a time of swift social change.

The central fact about the new workers is that they are young and bring into the plants with them the new perspectives of American youth in 1970. At the beginning of this year, roughly one-third of the hourly employees at Chrysler, General Motors, and Ford were under thirty. More than half of Chrysler's hourly workers had been there less than five years. The new workers have had more years in school, if not more of what a purist would call education: blue-collar workers between twenty-five and forty-four years old have completed twelve years of school, compared to ten years for those forty-five to sixty-four. It doesn't sound like much of a difference, but it means an increase of 20 percent. The new attitudes cut across racial lines. Both young blacks and young whites have higher expectations of the jobs they fill and the wages they receive, and for the lives they will lead. They are restless, changeable, mobile, demanding, all traits that make for impermanence — and for difficult adjustment to an assembly line. The deep dislike of the job and the desire to escape become terribly clear twice each day when shifts end and the men stampede out the plant gates to the parking lots, where they sometimes actually endanger lives in their desperate haste to be gone.

For management, the truly dismaying evidence about new worker attitudes is found in job performance. Absenteeism has risen sharply; in fact it has doubled over the past ten years at General Motors and at Ford, with the sharpest climb in the past year. It has reached the point where an average of 5 percent of G.M.'s hourly workers are missing from work without explanation every day. Moreover, the companies have seen only a slight dip in absenteeism since car production started declining last spring and layoffs at the plants began. On some days, notably Fridays and Mondays, the figure goes as high as 10 percent. Tardiness has increased, making it even more difficult to start up the production lines promptly when a shift begins — after the foreman has scrambled around to replace missing workers. Complaints about quality are up sharply. There are more arguments with fore-men, more complaints about discipline and overtime, more grievances. There is more turnover. The quit rate at Ford last year was 25.2 percent (this does not mean one worker in four quit, but simply that there was very heavy turnover among a small but volatile fraction, primarily of the younger ones). Some assembly-line workers are so turned off, mana-gers report with astonishment, that they just walk away in mid-shift and don't even come back to get their pay for time they have worked.

The result of all this churning labor turmoil is, in-evitably, wasted manpower, less efficiency, higher costs, a need for more inspections and repairs, more warranty claims — and grievous damage to company reputations as angry con-sumers rage over flaws in their glistening but all too fre-quently defective new cars. In some plants worker discontent has reached such a degree that there has been overt sabotage. Screws have been left in brake drums, tool handles welded into fender compartments (to cause mysterious, unfindable, and eternal rattles), paint scratched, and upholstery cut.

General Motors has taken the initiative in bringing the problem out into the open. . . . In his Christmas message to G.M.'s 794,000 employees, Chairman James Roche laid into those workers who "reject responsibility" and who "fail to respect essential disciplines and authority." He hit harder, and attracted wide attention, in a speech celebrating G.M.'s fiftieth anniversary in St. Louis. "Management and the pub-lic have lately been shortchanged," he said bluntly. "We have a right to more than we have been receiving." G.M. had increased its investment per hourly employee from $5,000 in 1950 to $24,000 in 1969, he said, "but tools and technology mean nothing if the worker is absent from his job." He stressed the domino effect of absenteeism on co-workers, on efficiency, on quality, and on other G.M. plants with related production. "We must receive the fair day's work for which we pay the fair day's wage."

The problem was thus clearly enunciated. The trouble is no one is really certain why the absentees are absent, why the tardies are tardy, why the discontented are discontent. It *is* known that the great majority of the hourly workers are reasonably faithful in attendance and that chronic absenteeism is concentrated among only 10 to 15 percent of the employees at each plant. It is these regularly irregular performers who have made the absentee rate jump to double the former figure; some of them miss one or more days each week.

The reasons they give cover the predictable stumbling blocks of life: car wouldn't start, wife sick, alarm clock didn't go off. Some candidly cite pressing amorous engagements that preclude their appearance at the plant. Doctors' certificates are popular because when absence is for a proved medical cause, pay is not docked. As a result, there is a thriving market for stolen prescription pads from doctors' offices — and medical excuses are viewed with skepticism. One personnel man called a doctor to check on an excuse the physician had written, and the doctor, misunderstanding the purpose of the call, assured the official, "Sure, send me anyone you got. I'll fix them up for five bucks apiece."

Absenteeism is notably higher on the less desirable late shifts, where there are more of the newer and younger employees. Lacking any precise knowledge of why the absentees stay away, beyond their often feeble excuses, the conclusion has to be that by staying out they are saying they don't like the job. The reasons for this are not yet known precisely either, but there are some useful clues.

First, it is significant that the absentee problem is especially severe in the automobile industry, where unskilled and thus less motivated workers constitute 70 percent of the labor force, compared to an average of only 10 percent unskilled in all industry. Automobile manufacturing is an old, entrenched industry with old, ultrasimplified methods originally designed not only to avoid waste motion but to accommodate unschooled immigrant labor and farm youths. It has a lot of old-line executives who have worked their way up for thirty and forty years. These men are used to dealing with engineers and machines in absolutes, not with fragile contemporary psyches. They tend to see the problem in basic terms, distrusting theorists and social scientists who claim the work is "monotonous" and "lacking in motivation factors." Earl Bramblett, the G.M. vice president for personnel, says absenteeism occurs not because the jobs are dull, but because of the nation's economic abundance, and the high degree of security and the many social benefits the industry provides. He cites the impressive gains labor has made and deplores the younger workers' insistence on even more benefits and improvements, thinks instead they should show more appreciation for what they have. At the, same time, too, top management is well aware that the young recruits, coming from today's more permissive homes and schools, often get their first real experience with discipline on the factory floor.

Further, the automobile industry lacks the relative glamour, the involvement and satisfaction of newer industrial jobs such as those at Polaroid or Texas Instruments or I.B.M. It seems fairly certain that, given a choice, most young auto workers would prefer jobs in those future-oriented firms. Automobile making is paced, in most of its production operations, by the inexorable demands of the assembly line, usually turning out about fifty-five cars per hour, leaving the men no flexibility of rhythm. At some plants there are sternly detailed work rules that would make a training sergeant at a Marine boot camp smile with pleasure. The rules prohibit such offenses as catcalls, horseplay, making preparations to leave work before the signal sounds, littering, wasting time, or loitering in toilets.

Another special handicap for the carmakers is that they are tied to big-city areas by their capital investments and their reliance on the inner city for a large pool of unskilled labor. Working conditions in the plants, some of which are gloomy and old, do not match those in many other industries; the setting is often noisy, dirty, even smelly, and some jobs carry health hazards. The pace of the line and the separation of work stations limit the amount of morale-sustaining camaraderie that can develop. The fact that 100,000 of the 740,000 auto workers were laid off for varying periods in 1970 has, of course, added to discontent.

In this rather somber setting it is hardly surprising that the injection of tens of thousands of hopeful young workers during recent years has caused some conflict. They both know more and expect more. Many have never experienced economic want or fear — or even insecurity. In the back of their minds is the knowledge that public policy will not allow them to starve, whatever may happen.

Walter Reuther pondered the industry's problem with youth in an educational-television interview a few weeks before his death. Young workers, he said, get three or four days' pay and figure, "Well, I can live on that. I'm not really interested in these material things anyhow. I'm interested in a sense of fulfillment as a human being." The prospect of tightening up bolts every two minutes for eight hours for thirty years, he said, "doesn't lift the human spirit." The young worker, said Reuther, feels "he's not master of his own destiny. He's going to run away from it every time he gets a chance. That is why there's an absentee problem."

The visual evidence of a new youthful individuality is abundant in the assembly plants. Along the main production line and in the subassembly areas there are beards; and shades, long hair here, a peace medallion there, occasionally some beads — above all, young faces, curious eyes. Those eyes have watched carefully as dissent has spread in the nation. These men are well aware that bishops, soldiers, diplomats, even Cabinet officers, question orders these days and dispute commands. They have observed that demonstrations and dissent have usually been rewarded. They do not look afraid, and they don't look as though they would take much guff. They are creatures of their times.

Management has tended to assume that good pay with a good fringe is enough to command worker loyalty and performance. For some, it is. General Motors has issued to all its workers an elaborate brochure informing them that even its lowest-paid hourly employees are in the top third of the U. S. income spectrum. (The average weekly wage at G.M. is $184.60.) But absenteeism continues, and learned theoreticians take issue with the automobile executives about money as a reward, arguing that men work for more than pay and that their other psychological needs must be satisfied.

Since pay alone demonstrably does not work, management must study the lessons offered by absenteeism, just as others have had to study the lessons of campus and political dissent among youth. One of the first things management must learn to do, as college presidents and politicians have had to learn, is to listen.

What the managers will hear is a rumbling of deep discontent and, particularly from young production workers, hostility to and suspicion of management. A black worker, twenty-two years old, at Ford in Dearborn, says he dislikes "the confusion between the workers and the supervisor." By "confusion" he means arguments. He would like to set his own pace: "It's too fast at times." The job is "boring, monotonous," there is "no glory"; he feels he is "just a number." He would not want to go any faster, he says, "not even for incentive pay." A white repair man in the G.M. assembly plant in Baltimore, twenty-nine years old, says, "Management tries to get more than a man is capable of. It cares only about production."

A black assembly worker at Chrysler who shows up for work regularly and at twenty-four, after Army service, gets $7,400-a-year base pay, says, "I don't like nothin' best about that job. It really ain't much of a job. The bossman is always on our backs to keep busy."

Talks with dozens of workers produced few words of praise for management. There is cynicism about possibilities for advancement. "Promotion depends on politics in the plant," a twenty-seven-year-old trim worker for Ford said, and others expressed similar views. "They tell you to do the job the way it's wrote, even if you find a better way," says an assembly worker, thirty-two, at Cadillac.

Complaints about the lack of time for personal business recurred in different plants. "You're tied down. You do the same thing every day, day in, day out, hour after hour," says a union committeeman, thirty-one, who worked on the line twelve years. "You're like in a jail cell — except they have more time off in prison. You can't do personal things, get a haircut, get your license plates, make a phone call." With the increased complexity of life, including more administrative and reporting obligations, more license and permit requirements, more insurance and medical and school forms, workers tied to the production line have difficulty keeping up. Unable even to phone in many cases, as their white-collar brethren can, they feel frustrated, and one result is they sometimes take a whole absentee day off to accomplish a simple half-hour chore. The problem affects everyone similarly, but here as in other areas of discontent, the young workers are quicker to complain, and more vociferous.

A prominent and somewhat surprising complaint is that companies have required too much overtime. Workers, particularly the younger ones with fewer responsibilities, want more free time and want to be able to *count* on that time. Overtime diminished or disappeared after the slowdown this year, but it will again become a problem when demand for cars increases. U.A.W. Vice President Douglas A. Fraser says, "In some cases high absenteeism has been caused almost exclusively by high overtime. The young workers won't accept the same old kind of discipline their fathers did." They dispute the .corporations' right to make them work overtime without their consent, he says, feeling this infringes on their individuality and freedom. Fraser recommends overtime be optional, not mandatory.

The foremen, as the most direct link between management and the workers, draw heavy criticism, most of it from the younger men. They are accused, variously and not always fairly, of too close supervision, of inattention or indifference, of riding and harassing men, of failing to show them their jobs adequately.

A young apprentice diemaker at Fisher Body says, "They could let you do the job your way. You work at it day after day. They don't." A General Motors worker in Baltimore, twenty-nine and black, says, "The foremen could show more respect for the workers — talk to them like men, not dogs. When something goes wrong, the foreman takes it out on the workers, who don't have nobody to take it out on."

There is also an increasing number of complaints by whites alleging favoritism or indulgence by foremen toward blacks — and similar complaints by blacks about whites. However, open clashes along racial lines are rare, even though blacks now constitute around 20 percent of the hourly force (varying by geographical location). The liberal leadership of the U.A.W. has a powerful influence on attitudes and as a result bigotry is generally concealed, if not eliminated. But black workers in some plants do tend to stick to themselves, and it is not uncommon for a black to converse by shouts with a brother twenty feet down the line rather than with the white across from him and only a yard away.

The more serious split that has developed in the plants is between the young and old. The tendency of the younger men to speak out rather than bottle up their grievances is contagious, and the older men, too, complain more than in the past. In this contentious atmosphere, young turn on old, and old on young. A young apprentice diemaker at Fisher Body says, "The older guys sit back and take it easy, because they got their time in. They razz the kids a little." A Baltimore worker denounces older men for catering to the company: "They do all they can to follow instructions when the company tries one more speedup."

Some of the older workers are just as bitter. A forty-three-year-old diemaker is angry at the diminished sense of craftsmanship among the young. "They make me sick," he says, adding angrily that a third-year apprentice he knows, "who is a dummy," is making only $300 a year less than he is. Another says, "The older men feel the young are cocky, that they better watch themselves." A thirty-eight-year-old worker on the Cadillac transmission line says flatly, "I resent the younger ones. They feel they should come in and not take turn in seniority — they want the big jobs right away."

The antagonism between young and old, although by no means universal, is reflected in union affairs as well. The union leadership is of another generation, and some of the younger workers feel they are a constituency without a voice. They are suspicious of what they see as close ties between union delegates and management. A Baltimore Chevrolet worker, twenty-nine and black, says, "Sometimes it looks like the company and the union had gotten together on a matter when maybe they shouldn't."

The morale of the young workers is summed up grimly by Frank E. Runnels, the thirty-five-year-old president of U.A.W. Local 22 at Cadillac: "Every single unskilled young man in that plant wants out of there. They just don't like it." Runnels, who put in thirteen years on the assembly line, says there has been a sharp increase in the use of drugs and that heavy drinking is a continuing problem. "This whole generation has been taught by their fathers to avoid the production line, to go to college to escape, and now some of them are trapped. They can't face it; they hate to go in there."

Much of the blame for present problems goes to industry managers who have done little to make the jobs more rewarding. "They haven't tried to build motivators into the jobs," says the Reverend E. Douglas White, associate director of the Detroit Industrial Mission, a labor counseling group. Gene Brook, director of labor education at Wayne State University, blames the young auto workers' anger on "the guy's feeling that he is not a part of anything," that he is an interchangeable cog in the production process. "Workers who want a sense of self-development, and want to contribute," says management consultant Stanley Peterfreund, "instead are made to feel unimportant." Campus and factory ferment have similar origins, in the opinion of Fred K. Foulkes, an assistant professor at the Harvard Graduate School of Business Administration. "People want more control, more autonomy. They want to be the acting agent rather than acted upon." Foulkes, author of *Creating More Meaningful Work,* stresses that the discipline of the assembly line adds a special problem. "People *have* to be there," he says. "There's no relief until relief time comes around. The whole situation, therefore, is inconsistent with what seems to be going on in society — and it's too costly to change the technology. So the question remains: How do you permit men to be individuals?"

John Gardner, in his new book *The Recovery of Confidence,* says, in an observation that might have been crafted to order for the automobile business, "An important thing to understand about any institution or social system is that it doesn't move until it's pushed." The push applied to the carmakers has been the sharp surge of absenteeism, dissension, and shoddy workmanship in their plants. Admittedly, the industry managers are hampered in their efforts to meet the demands, spoken and unspoken, of their youthful new employees because they are boxed in by the givens within which they operate. The old plants, the urban setting, the tyranny of the assembly line, all make solutions more difficult. But the industry has become increasingly aware of the problems facing it, has considered a wide variety of approaches, and is moving ahead on several of them.

One attack is being made at the level where management and hourly workers meet, on the plant floor, through the foremen. On the average there is one foreman to thirty production workers, and the majority of foremen have come up from the hourly ranks themselves. All of the big three auto companies operate training programs for foremen designed to increase their effectiveness as leaders. Pontiac takes foremen off on weekends to various resorts for specially tailored sensitivity training and discussion of the problems new workers face. At Chrysler a special consultant instructs foremen on the difficulties black workers encounter when starting work in an auto plant.

Since late in 1968, General Motors has operated a "New Work Force" program for foremen in plants across the country. The title was chosen to indicate General Motors' awareness that there is indeed a new and different work force, not so homogeneous as in the past, including blacks and whites, old and young, persons with little education and of various cultures, some with criminal records, many who would once have been considered unemployable. The program gives managers a look at the lives of such workers, takes them into ghetto areas, puts them in role-playing situations in which they act out the workers' parts in orientation and disciplinary interviews. Supervisors are shown how to reduce new employees' tensions, feelings that if unresolved can cause a new man to quit, stay away from work, or rebel in some other fashion. Ford, too, conducts human-relations programs at various plants to guide supervisors in dealing with motivation, work, control, costs, and quality.

Some of the foremen have been hard to convince, particularly those who have been threatened with violence or even death (such threats are not uncommon in connection with firings, according to the foremen). But the message about the need for a new approach is getting through. Reflecting the change, one chassis-assembly foreman at Cadillac said, "I try to work *with* them, not threaten them. The old-type tactics of being a supervisor don't work with these guys." A foreman in Pontiac's foundry division said, "I try not to use the discipline route. I tell the man the pocketbook effect on him. Some of this absenteeism is for simple reasons, like the foreman didn't smile right or turned his back when you were talking. Or family reasons, the wife is sick." He gets questioned on assignments, he says, "but I try to anticipate the questions and explain why. That way, if he wants to argue he has to meet me head on."

General Motors runs a vigorous, well-financed suggestion program as a way of creating and sustaining employee initiative. Last year 324,647 ideas came in and the company paid out more than $17 million for the 279,461 suggestions adopted. Ford has just put into distribution to its plants a new film in *cinéma verité* style aimed at new employees. It is designed to show them what production work is really like, so that when they step out on the clangorous floor on that first day of work they won't be dismayed. It has an unusual title, *Don't Paint It Like Disneyland,* and, as a Ford official said, "It's an unusual industrial film. We don't have the chairman of the board giving a speech about working for Ford, either at the beginning or at the end." It is unusual, too, in its candor. In it one production worker says, "It's a drag at first, but you realize you got to do it; so you do it." Another looks up from his job on the line and says in a puzzled way, "I got a good job — but it's pretty bad."

Ford is also looking hard for ways to give workers more feeling of responsibility and authority in their work. One tactic being applied to all Ford assembly plants is an established technique with a new name. It is called the "positive-buy" inspection. The inspector puts his initials on the inspection sheet for each car he passes. This indicates personal approval and ensures active examination rather than passive acceptance. Various plant managers are experimenting with other motivational approaches such as job rotation, group or team work, and self-set quotas, but they are hampered by the inflexible nature of the automobile-assembly process, and by the reluctance of many workers to change familiar routines.

At the Chevrolet assembly plant in Baltimore, where absenteeism has gone up steadily from just over 3 percent in 1966 to 7.5 percent in 1970, management is trying a whole array of tactics. The basic approach there, too, is through the foremen, who are told to make every effort to know their workers as individuals and to try to make them *want* to do their jobs. Workers needing time off for personal business are urged to ask in advance, so that management can plan ahead to replace them. The problem here is that not all such requests can be granted — not everyone can leave during Maryland's deer season, for example — and refusal can create more resentment.

The next stage beyond motivation is what Baltimore plant management terms "the discipline route." Workers and union officials say that there has been a definite "tightening of the reins," including more reprimands, more "time off" (meaning disciplinary suspension without pay), and more dismissals. One Friday on the second shift (three-thirty to midnight) more than 200 employees were absent, out of the shift force of 2,700 hourly workers. Management decided to shut down the plant after four hours, a decision that meant those who had come to work lost half a day's pay, through no fault of their own. The union cried foul, claiming management took the absenteeism as a money-saving excuse to cut production because of lower sales. To get back at management, dozens of workers canceled their savings-bond and community-chest deductions, both ardently advocated by the company.

Plant manager H. H. Prentice had letters mailed to every worker, addressed "Dear Fellow-employee and Family," explaining why the closing was necessary, urging "your best effort in being at work every day on time," and expressing certainty that "most of our employees want to be at work every day to provide for themselves and their families." Thus to the "discipline route" was added "the family route." With cooperation from employees, Prentice ended, "we will avoid the necessity of harsh disciplinary measures." The threat seemed sufficiently clear.

Two quite sweeping methods have been suggested by various managers and theoreticians for dealing once and for all with worker discontent. One is to keep the jobs as dull as they are, and hire dull men to fill them. This seems a backward-looking course at best, even if such a large, docile labor force still existed anywhere in this country. At the other extreme are the proposals for automating the plants completely, throwing out the old assembly line in the process, and eliminating the dull jobs altogether. Unfortunately, this solution is not feasible either with present technology.

The more central course, which many advocate, would have managers find ways to make the jobs varied and interesting through both motivation and technology. The industry is certainly looking. On the motivational side, some G.M. plants have even tried rewarding regular attendance with Green Stamps, or initialed drinking glasses. G.M. took some long steps toward more complete automation in planning for production of its low-cost Vega 2300. The production line, built at Lordstown, Ohio, was designed to permit assembling a hundred cars per hour, compared with the usual fifty-five, and surpassing even the ninety-one Oldsmobiles built each hour at Lansing. Since labor input must be reduced if G.M. is to make a profit building these smaller, cheaper cars, every phase of the assembly operation is being restudied and much of it is being redesigned. For example, the Vega chassis will be raised and lowered automatically as it moves along the line, to speed assembly and make the workers' jobs easier.

Whatever is done, says G.M.'s director of employee research, Delmar L. Landen, Jr., it must be remembered that absenteeism and allied production problems are only symptoms of the trouble. For too long the automobile industry has "assumed economic man was served if the pay was okay," says Landen, who has a doctorate in industrial psychology and fourteen years experience with G.M. "It didn't matter if the job was fulfilling. Once the pay is good, though, higher values come into play." Other satisfactions are required. "One thing is sure: if they won't come in for $32.40 a day, they won't come in for a monogrammed glass." In Landen's view, a greater sense of participation must be built into the job; he does not know just how. He is completing a major survey of foremen to learn the exact dimensions of, and the basic reasons for, low worker morale. From the findings, he will develop specific recommendations. At this point he is surprisingly optimistic. "We are having very vital, critical changes in our society," he says. "And the question is how we can capitalize on this, how we can exploit the forces of change and profit from them."

Nobody disputes that these new workers are the brightest, best-educated labor force that ever came into the plants. If their potential were somehow fully released, they would be an asset instead of a problem. But it is clear, too, that solutions will not be quick and easy. A new challenge to the industry has quite clearly been thrown down. Old familiar plants that once taught industrial efficiency to the world have, almost unnoticed, undergone a change of season. In the new climate young workers have created, top management must increasingly think of its workers and the satisfactions they can and should derive from their work. Failure to do so would mean failure, ultimately, in management's basic responsibilities to its stockholders as well.

Young Blacks vs. the Work World

by Dennis Derryck

The seventies find blacks still suffering from many of the inequities that have long been associated with minority status in this country, inequities that have been especially persistent in the area of employment. The unemployment rate for blacks is double the white rate. The relative income of blacks has decreased, when compared to whites, to the point that the median income of black families with three earners is not significantly different from that of white families with only one earner. In addition, American society's great equalizer, the public education system, has been revealed to be a myth in terms of what it has provided blacks. The reality is that the public schools have blatantly and massively failed to educate blacks as a group. What data exists regarding improvement in the median years of schooling completed by blacks loses much of its meaning when the quality of the education blacks have received is examined.

This paper will limit its discussion to young black workers, age twenty to thirty, with a high school diploma or less. To understand their attitudes toward work, we must not only consider the inequalities in employment rates, earnings and education just mentioned, but must likewise place these facts within the context of the promises and hopes of 1954, and the promises and hopes of the civil rights movement. There are many complex psychological factors involved in black attitudes toward work. These factors, though crucial inputs into the work gestalt, to a large extent have not yet been quantified. Indeed, very little analysis relative to our subject

Reprinted with permission from *New Generation*. Copyright © 1970 by the National Committee on Employment of Youth.

has been carried out from a black perspective such as the one adopted here. Motivational studies based on the white, Protestant ethic have never been fully valid for blacks — and will be increasingly less so in the future. Among the psychological factors that must be considered are the externalization-internalization conflict, discrimination, the role of salary, urban-rural differences among blacks, the qualification syndrome and social relevancy.

The externalization-internalization conflict is a direct outgrowth of the civil rights movement of the sixties which sparked the development of black awareness, confidence and pride. While blacks won many of their legal rights, the result can best be described as the winning by blacks of access which was not matched by the winning of real assets.

This set up what I call the externalization-internalization conflict. Externally, blacks still face real, if subtler, forms of discrimination: their housing remains poor and so does their education; they continue to be the last hired. Externally, blacks expressed their frustration through the cry for black power and riots. The evolution of the system of inequalities now moved from individual racism to institutional racism, as is documented by the Kerner Report. Note that *The Profile of the Rioter* indicated that the average black person involved in the riots was a high school graduate and did have a "decent job." In recent years the black community has begun to express a vote of no confidence in the institutions of this society. For a growing number of young blacks the world of work seems to be included in this rejection.

While the true meaning of the internalization process may be debatable, and the degree of rhetoric involved unknown, the fact remains that internalization does exist. It can be measured by the growth of black organizations within the community and an increased reliance on black community unity for the solution of problems. Young blacks, particularly, have internalized the cultural emphasis on black pride and self-respect. Inevitably, this has begun to be reflected in their attitudes toward jobs and work.

Integration, accepted as a primary social goal by an older

generation of blacks, takes on a different meaning under the impact of what I have called the externalization-internalization conflict — heightened expectations and self-awareness versus pervasive, unacknowledged discrimination. When a young black applies for work with an "equal opportunity employer" and sees only token blacks in menial positions, he is subjected to an even more agonizing ego-assault than the straightforward segregation of earlier periods. (Some estimates indicate that as many as 60 per cent of working blacks are underemployed.) Assimilation into such a work world may well appear to contradict, rather than foster, his aspirations.

Young blacks in such a situation will increasingly reject the assimilated work ethic of their parents' generation. They tend to prefer work within the black community, when this is available. Recent cutbacks in federal funds for community action have deprived many young blacks of such an outlet for their discontent. Another expression of the same conflict is growing militancy among younger black employees. This may be most dramatically exemplified in the auto industry by groups like DRUM, FRUM, CRUM — Dodge/Ford/Chrysler, etc., Revolutionary Union Movements. These unions within the union show every indication of growing militancy on behalf of their black members.

A simplistic approach which assumes that this generation of blacks can be pacified by high wage jobs is naive. Such an argument is contradicted by the continuing role of job discrimination against blacks in society, the nature of the jobs available to blacks, the young black worker's perception of the job, and his problems of vocational choice.

Discrimination still looms as a major factor that blacks must face. Equal Employment Opportunity Commission data for New York City indicated that, if we dig deeper than citywide aggregate figures for private employment, we find that total exclusion of minorities from white-collar jobs was by no means uncommon. In 1968, of the 4,249 reporting establishments in New York City, 1,151 (27 per cent) did not employ a single black in any capacity and 1,827 (43 per cent) had no black employees at the white-collar level. Fourteen of the largest twenty white-collar industries had participation rates below the city-wide average of 6.3 per cent for blacks.

Despite these inequities, the economic boom of the sixties assured some kind of job for the majority of blacks who wished to work. Data on those assisted by manpower programs indicated that many had a work history before coming to the programs. In general, however, the quality of the jobs available to them was poor. If salary was taken to be the major consideration, it would have to be admitted that decent paying jobs for blacks were in reality very scarce. A beginning was made in such industries as construction and printing, but even though such industries train an important segment for future managerial positions, they train relatively few in terms of society's needs, much less of the black community's needs. For example, the largest printing union in the country accepted no more than twenty blacks between 1964 and 1969. High salaried opportunities for the non-college black were very limited. For the majority of blacks, jobs that paid well were not readily available. Clearly, this had its greatest impact on young workers or those entering the work force.

To conceive high salaries as the sole criterion of job choice or satisfaction on the part of these young black workers is unrealistic on other grounds as well. High-wage white workers who are dissatisfied with the content of their jobs can view their earnings as means to a better life and therefore as some compensation for the emptiness of their work. (This arrangement is increasingly less acceptable to young white workers as well.) This generation of blacks, however, must face the fact that even higher earnings merely perpetuate a system that offers them no real improvements; their earnings go to maintain continued poor education and the purchase of inferior quality goods in their community. Escalating turnover rates among young blacks who have been able to obtain better paying jobs indicate the fallacy of a simplistic high-wage approach.

If job choice were a completely rational process, black attitudes toward the world of work could be more accurately analyzed. But for most blacks, entry into the work world is largely controlled by what is available and by chance. Those who are fortunate enough to obtain a well-paid position through chance may have to face difficult psychological adjustments. On a newly integrated job, isolation (defined as being the sole black in a position) can be devastating. If the job, however, does meet certain personal psychological needs, then the irrationality of the vocational choice will not be too disturbing. I recall the number of blacks who quickly volunteered to become ironworkers in the construction industry in New York City with beginning wages of $4.25 per hour. For most it really did not matter what the nature of the work was, and most had little or no knowledge of what the job might entail. Their basic consideration was that at such wages basic personal needs could be satisfied. Of the first ten blacks referred to the ironworkers job, not one survived a week on the job.

Irrational vocational choices due to a lack of knowledge of opportunities may not always result in such an immediate turnover rate, but high turnover rates are indicative of the dissatisfaction of blacks with the work world.

Discrimination, however, has complex ramifications beyond the outright limitation of the jobs open to blacks. A study of black applicants studying for entrance into a sheet-metal workers' apprenticeship program indicated that success in passing the examination was less closely associated with achievement or I.Q. than with the extent of discrimination the individual perceived. Those who were successful in passing the examination perceived the construction industry and the union as being open to all, as non-discriminating. Moreover, they tended to feel they had never been discriminated against in their lives. The attitude of black workers toward their jobs will be influenced by the manner in which they perceive discrimination.

How a job is perceived by the black community and the white community often plays an important part in young blacks' attitudes toward specific types of work. Sanitation work is an example of these dynamics in operation. In some urban areas of the country this job is highly prized, whereas in others the opposite is true. Frequently, this perception has a racial basis. The racial mix of those employed in a particular occupation is frequently important and may well determine society's attitudes, and particularly black attitudes, toward a specific type of work. There is a need for further study of the changing attitudes of blacks and the larger society as a specific occupation changes its racial mix. How the stigma of a "black job" (nigger work) operates psychologically is something about which we know very little. The usual view is, unfortunately, that any work dominated by blacks cannot be very good. This perception creates a conflict for the young black seeking employment. On one hand he will be drawn to jobs like bank clerk or teller, where the work is clean and he wears a jacket and tie. This seems to indicate a breaking away from the dirty, menial work available to his father's generation. On the other hand, the low wages and absence of advancement possibilities for this group of workers remind them forcefully of how limiting and limited such jobs are.

There can be no doubt that contrasts in work attitudes exist between young blacks raised in urban centers and those who migrate to the cities from rural areas. For a certain period, the latter will be less aware of the pervasive job discrimination I have described and will feel less frustration. The facts indicate an ironic parallel with Klineberg's study, *Negro Intelligence and Selective Migration,* made in the 1930's and now outdated. His study indicated that it took an average of eight years for blacks who migrated from the South into northern schools to be able to improve their I.Q.'s to equal those of urban blacks. Something similar is now taking place in terms of work attitudes and frustration. After a few years of working for unattainable goals in urban centers, the rural-born black exhibits a sense of frustration and a perception of job discrimination equal to his urban-born brother.

Job qualifications based on formal education rather than on ability or job performance are, in many ways, an influential factor in black attitudes toward work. While the qualifications syndrome is closely associated with management's policy concerning promotion, the reality is that only a small percentage of workers are actually ever promoted. It is also true that educational achievement as measured by years of schooling is not directly correlated with the quality of jobs available or with the quality of job performance. The proportions of this situation are indicated in a Bureau of Labor Statistics special report on the employment experience of youth not in school in October, 1969. The report states:

". . . over twice as many Negro as white high school graduates in the labor force were unemployed. For Negro youth, educational achievement did not seem to be the determining factor in the likelihood of unemployment; Negro graduates had about the same unemployment rate as Negro dropouts (15.8 per cent and 18.1 per cent, respectively). Other factors such as job discrimination, quality of schooling, and geographic location appear to play a part in the relatively high unemployment of young Negro graduates.

"In comparing occupations by race, it was found that Negro graduates tended to hold less prestigious jobs requiring less skill and training and probably providing less pay than the white high school graduates. . . . About three-fourths of the Negroes, but only one-half of the young white men, were employed as operatives, nonfarm laborers, or in service occupations" (*Monthly Labor Review,* August 1970) .

The frustration caused by this situation is aggravated by the young black worker's realization that his white supervisors or whites in higher level jobs are not really performing tasks that are difficult, nor tasks beyond the range of his own ability. He may well interpret this phenomenon as a perpetuation of racist discrimination. Another closely connected source of work frustration is the general supposition that jobs with upward mobility produce greater job satisfaction and less turnover. But for the black with a high school education or less, upward mobility on the job is a rare piece of luck, indeed.

Several factors make it very difficult to hypothesize about the future of young blacks in the work world. The immediate prospects do not offer much basis for optimism. The young black workers we have been discussing and those who will follow them will undoubtedly feel mounting frustration and resentment. The internalization process will certainly continue, indeed accelerate, and will conflict increasingly harshly with their perception of racist discrimination in terms of the availability and desirability of jobs. All of the characteristics of American society that assault the well-being and dignity of all blacks will weigh most heavily on the young. Their attitudes toward work and their behavior on the job will certainly be affected by their growing militancy.

Young blacks see that most unions have done little or nothing for them in terms of higher paying jobs. They will be increasingly militant toward white co-workers and union leaders. The pattern of a black "union within a union," described above regarding the auto industry, will undoubtedly spread. Industries that continue to be misled by the fallacy of high wages will see increased turnover among black workers as well as mounting problems in their plants. Manpower programs that deal with increasing the number of jobs without improving the quality of the jobs will fail. Band-aid approaches like sensitivity training have already proved futile, because they aim only at manipulating the symptoms of the problem. Since it seems highly improbable that the public and private sectors of our society will mobilize the massive change of direction that is needed, the future will be more full of conflict and bitterness than the present.

A New Breed of Manager

by Nathan Glassman

The changing work ethic is not exclusively observed in Detroit auto factories and Pittsburgh steel mills. The corridors of corporate management are increasingly peopled by young men of a different stamp from W. H. Whyte's "organization man." There has always been at least limited tolerance in the corporate structure for the maverick, the nonconforming individualist, provided his abilities made him sufficiently valuable to the organization. The present difference is that rejection of traditional standards of job behavior is emerging as the hallmark of an important number of young businessmen. The highly fluid behavior and attitudes generally, if somewhat amorphously, associated with the "youth culture" are making themselves felt in corporate life.

The traditional entry job in the corporate structure insulated a man from significant decision-making for from three to ten years and then gradually allowed him to approach the "levers" of power. During this protracted novitiate the efficiency and devotion to duty of the junior executive were observed by his superiors, whose authority lay largely beyond question. Graduates presently entering the management world are adamantly unwilling to accept such a situation. Better educated than earlier generations, they are completely unsympathetic to long-term training programs that seem nothing more than additional schoolwork. They want — and indeed, demand — relevant and significant jobs from the beginning of their career. If such jobs are not assigned them, they are very inclined to leave the company and look elsewhere.

Reprinted with permission from *New Generation*. Copyright © 1970 by the National Committee on Employment of Youth.

(Turnover rates among young men in their first two years of work may reach as high as 150 per cent.)

There is no good reason to think this trend will reverse itself, even though occasionally it may be temporarily modified by general economic pressures. The change appears permanent, with profound social and cultural roots. Today's corporate recruits are not children of the depression; they are not fixated on economic security. Neither is their primary work interest the externally determined status level of their job. From the outset, they refuse to allow the corporation or their superior to stand *in loco parentis,* as a substitute father with proprietary and unquestioned authority. They understand themselves as adults and demand to be treated as such on the job. The emerging pattern indicates that today's young management candidate has internalized work values that accord with his personal aspirations rather than with extrinsic considerations of security and status.

It is important to clarify what is signified by the desire for "relevance" in terms of work. As a rule, the young manager seeks a *personal,* as distinct from *social,* relevance in his job. He demands, in other words, that the job substantially match the idea he has of himself and the sense of achievement that he considers a value. Within the range of his aspirations and expectations he is open to a number of possibilities. He is willing to make what he considers a reasonable adjustment to the demands of the job or the corporate structure. He is definitely not willing to make a complete, one-sided adjustment.

The constant ingredient amid all the variations in this phenomenon is the demand for authentic work and for responsibility on the job. This psychological need is intensified by the lengthening separation between the age of reaching maturity — physiologically as well as socially — and the age when young people are admitted to adult roles. This may explain why the work-related behavior and attitudes under discussion are so pervasive. They are in evidence among the short- and the long-haired, the squares and the swingers, political conservatives and liberals. Even important differences among individuals do not lessen the wariness to the corporate organization felt by the young nor substantially modify the demands that they make.

The effects of this changed work ethic are only beginning to be felt in corporations, as younger men who share these attitudes begin to reach higher managerial positions. On the whole, the higher echelon managers are unaware of the real nature of what is happening. Because they find it difficult to understand how different from their own the younger men's experience has been, they are inclined to misinterpret their behavior. Too often, they take the symptoms, that is, the style that expresses the new attitude to work, as the total substance of what has changed and remain ignorant of the far more important underlying causes. Complaints that a young man "wants to be a vice-president in six months" miss the point that what he really wants is work that is real and a chance to express himself honestly.

These young men, products of an era and an educational system that have placed great emphasis on interpersonal dynamics, are frequently aware of the complicated human interaction between themselves and those in positions of authority. Their social experience has geared them to recognize the value and uses of power. As a result, their relationships to their elders and superiors are likely to be expressed in quasi-political terms.

Generally, the tension between youthful demand and upper echelon incomprehension does not reach an impasse. A number of relatively extrinsic considerations save the situation from a dead-center balance. The pressure on profits that even the largest corporations are presently experiencing has quite naturally led their policy-makers to exercise extreme care about overhead costs. One major consideration is necessarily a review of personnel and salary policies. In the interest of leaner organization, many corporations have moved to make entry jobs more human in order to increase productivity and to retain the services of their most talented younger men. Not from any explicitly humanitarian motive, but simply in order to promote efficiency, these corporations are gradually meeting the demands of their younger men for meaningful jobs. In the process, they are restructuring their managerial organization from the bottom.

Other factors are also at work to counter corporate inertia. Discontent with meaningless, dehumanizing jobs on the lower levels is beginning to spread upward to the middle management levels. Since men on the middle levels may be only a few years older than those below them, they can more readily understand and share their attitudes.

In addition, the corporation and its personnel cannot escape the pressures and trends of the general society. The drive toward personal autonomy, so broadly manifest in contemporary society, works subtly to change the habits and expectations of managers as well as of professors and students. The loosening of rigid social bonds — familial, cultural, ethical, political — necessarily exerts some influence on the authority relationships in corporations. Younger managers apparently no longer find it imperative that success result from harsh personal competition. Their primary motivation for accepting and performing a job is the satisfaction it affords their personal aspirations. The job will command their interest and energies to the degree that it answers their internalized needs. The emerging pattern indicates that there is no necessary conflict between organizational needs and personal needs.

The picture should not be oversimplified. Corporations still get many achievement-oriented types among their young management candidates, men who are uniquely suited to standard organizational behavior. On the other hand, the young men whose attitudes and behavior I have described do represent a threat to some of those on upper management levels. Whereas corporations used to "shelf" or pension off unproductive middle- or upper-level managers, today they can no longer afford this practice. Faced with a plentiful supply of better equipped and cheaper young men, they are more inclined simply to dismiss their unproductive elders. Shelf-sitting is being eliminated and the elaborate protective patterns of the past are being removed. Naturally, the shelf-sitters feel threatened by their young confreres.

The changed work-related attitudes and behavior of young managers is noticeably affecting the conception and organization of management training programs. These programs are intended to provide an examination and polishing period for the management candidate. His supervisors expect to determine his ability to be productive and to handle responsibility. They were also originally conceived as a safeguard against the errors inevitably committed by inexperienced men during their on-the-job training period. At present there is a several-pronged reaction against the lengthy training program. First of all, it did not eliminate error-making. For this and other reasons, corporations are moving back toward a policy of toleration for some mistakes. Secondly, technological change takes place so rapidly that the idea of training someone once and for all to meet complex responsibilities is unrealistic.

The third consideration, and the one of most interest within the context of this discussion, focuses on the attitudes and reactions of the trainees. There is a profound dissatisfaction among those entering business with spending a lengthy period — one or two years — as a trainee. They want an opportunity for full responsibility and productivity much earlier than was formerly allowed. The last thing the young graduate wants after sixteen or seventeen years of schooling is two more years as a pupil. In addition, there is considerable and widespread dissatisfaction with the training programs themselves. Many young men complain of the unsuitable and/or inconsequential jobs to which they are assigned, and of being ignored by their supervisors. Moreover, many trainees do not find the mechanics and objectives of the training program clearly defined. They do not know what they are being trained *for*. Thomas H. Patten, Jr., has written that "the likelihood that employees will not turnover rapidly hinges upon their being given assignments and movement that are perceived by them to be developmental."

Various reforms of training program procedures have been proposed or tried. They include such image-oriented measures as eliminating the term "trainee." But more substantial innovations are also emerging. In a time of rapid technological changes, some type of permanent or continuing education concept seems called for. This would entail short periods of training or retraining interspersed with shorter or longer periods of work. This pattern might well continue through most, or all, of a manager's career. Such a system would respond to the executive's desire for meaningful work and the organization's need to maximize productivity. It would also prevent an able manager from being bypassed by technological developments or by younger men trained in the new techniques.

Some corporations have instituted a "sponsor" system for training. The sponsor is usually not the new man's direct superior but is formally assigned to serve, in addition to his regular job, as his mentor and guide through the organizational complexity. In contrast to the quasi-parental status of the older type trainer, the sponsor is usually a near contemporary higher in rank. This arrangement emphasizes their personal relationship and thus avoids the stark organizational teacher-pupil ratio. There are many variations in the application of this approach even within a single organization. For example, the relationship tends to be less formal in research departments than in sales or production.

Other demands of young men entering management are also being met for reasons having little to do with changed work attitudes. Promotions tend to come more quickly than in the past largely because of business expansion. Corporations have to move young men into positions of responsibility faster.

The definitive commitment that used to be demanded by corporations and given by managers is gradually disappearing. The young manager does not feel any strong loyalty to the organization as such. As a general rule, he expects to change to another employer under a variety of quite easily foreseeable circumstances. He takes it for granted that he will work for a number of corporations in the course of his career. Transfers between departments within the same organization are also far more common and acceptable than they were. A young man in a job with which he is unhappy will ask for, and expect to receive, a transfer. One side benefit to the corporation is that unnecessary jobs are revealed in this way and can be eliminated.

Corporations are discovering that, far from being able to exist in a vacuum, they do not even exist in a world of their own making. Like all our major social institutions, they are influenced in myriad ways by the ebb and flow of events in the world around them. Even their internal structures are affected, subtly but profoundly, by the currents of change that mark American life. If society is being changed by a new generation with new standards, corporations will not escape untouched. Common sense would seem to dictate openness to the young and their demands. New forms of corporate organization will have to be devised to accommodate changed attitudes to work.

Women and Work

from *Work in America*

Housekeeping may still be the main occupation of American women, but it is no longer the only occupation or source of identity for most of them. In the past, a woman's sense of identity and main source of satisfaction centered on the husband's job, the home, and the family. Today, there are alternatives opening to increasing numbers of the female population. In addition to the fact that half of all women between the ages of 18 and 64 are presently in the labor force, Department of Labor studies have shown that 9 out of 10 women will work outside the home at some time in their lives. Increasingly, women of all ages are year-round, full-time members of the labor force. For many of these women, the traditional role played by work in the home is being supplemented or supplanted by work in the labor force. The following comment is probably not atypical for a working woman today:

> ...I had no confidence in myself, except at my job. I kept on feeling, if only I could find some missing element, I could enjoy cleaning house. But the whole thing is structured so that a woman loses her identity, so that she puts herself aside for another person. Men don't benefit either, but they don't lose so much. It was no problem for my husband. He didn't need to get his identity from our marriage. He got it from his job.

The women's movement has focused considerable attention on the role of work in life, and because of the kinds of dissatisfying jobs they have held traditionally, we can rea-

Reprinted from *Work in America,* Report of a Special Task Force to the Secretary of Health, Education, and Welfare; The MIT Press, 1973.

sonably expect women to be speaking out more forcefully on the quality of working life.

What is the quality of working life for women in the labor force? The job of secretary is perhaps symbolic of the status of female employment in this country, both qualitatively and quantitatively. There are 9 million secretaries and they compose nearly one-third of the nation's female workforce. Judy Klemesrud has written that the secretary is often stereotyped as a "gum-chewing sex kitten; husband hunter; miniskirted ding-a-ling; slow-witted pencil pusher; office go-fer ['go-fer coffee,' etc.]; reliable old shoe." Certainly, many secretaries have very poor jobs by the accepted standards of job satisfaction. Typists, in particular, have low status, little autonomy, little opportunity for growth, and receive low pay. In many instances (in typing pools, for example), the typist is viewed as little more than an appendage to the machine she operates. But the problems of women and work extend far beyond just this one often unrewarding job.

Much of the work that women currently do outside their homes deflates their self-images. The majority of the worst white-collar jobs probably are held by women: keypunch operators, telephone company operators, and clerical workers. Women are also over-represented on assembly-lines — the worst jobs in the economy. Yet, as the Michigan Survey of Working Conditions showed, women derive the same satisfaction as men do from the intrinsic rewards of work — when they are available. The Survey also found, however, that women are nearly twice as likely as men to express negative attitudes toward their present jobs. The cause of this dissatisfaction seems to lie in the discrepancy between women's high expectations about work and the actual low social and economic statuses of their jobs. Education is another important variable. A recent study of *The Quality of Life* shows that college educated women are most happy if they have jobs, and less happy if they don't (presumably because they tend to have more interesting jobs); married women without college educations are not necessarily less happy if they don't have jobs (presumably because of the less interesting jobs that are available to them).

One of the most pervasive and consequential of all cultural attitudes relating to sex concerns occupational sex-typing. Occupational sex-typing occurs when a large majority of those in an occupation are of one sex, and when there is an associated normative expectation that this is how things should be. Characteristics necessary for success in a sex-typed occupation become those associated with either a male or female role stereotype. Thus, occupations for women are found closely linked to their homemaking role; others to their socialization as men's helpmates. Conversely, occupations from which women are excluded tend to be those that involve "nonfeminine" pursuits or those that necessitate supervision of other employees. The result of these exclusionary practices is to crowd women into a limited number of jobs where the pressures of excess supply lower wages below the level that would otherwise prevail. Women become secretaries, schoolteachers, waitresses, and nurses, while men become plumbers, doctors, engineers, and school administrators. Once such a division of labor becomes established, it tends to be self-perpetuating since each sex is socialized, trained, and counseled into certain jobs and not into others.

The particular division of labor that emerges has little social or economic rationale. What is "man's work" in one period or place may become "woman's work" under different circumstances. For example, schoolteaching, telephone operating, and clerical work were once male occupations in the United States. More recently, the occupations of bank teller and school crossing guard have been feminized. In the Soviet Union, 79 percent of the doctors, 37 percent of the lawyers, 32 percent of the engineers, and 76 percent of the economists are female. Thus, cross-cultural and historical materials suggest that the present occupational structure does not reflect basic and unchanging differences in temperament or ability between the sexes. More important, a rather extensive body of evidence shows that the present division of labor is not the result of differences in the quality or the demographic composition of the male and female labor force. Nor are there important differences between working men and women where schooling, age, race, and geographical distributions are concerned.

There is some evidence that differences in earnings of men and women are quite large. In 1955, the average female employee earned 64 percent of the wages paid to a similarly employed man; and by 1970, she took home only 59 percent as much. This wage disparity is reflected in a more tangible sense in the figures for saleswork in the United States for 1970. In the sales field, women averaged $4,188 versus $9,790 earned by similarly employed salesmen. (A good part of this discrepancy is due to differences in proportion of year worked. For example, only 25 percent of women sales workers were employed full-year, full-time in 1969, as compared to 68 percent of male sales workers.)

While strides to correct pay discrepancies have been made through equal pay legislation, many economists dismiss the significance of this approach, pointing out that discrimination against women more often takes the form of job segregation rather than unequal pay; that is, women are being penalized not so much by being underpaid as by being underutilized. It is true that many married women are "secondary workers" in the sense that their income is additional to, and much smaller than, their husband's. Yet 86 percent of all working wives had husbands earning less than $10,000 per annum. In 1966, 61 percent had husbands earning less than $7,000. Most women work, then, for economic reasons, not just for "pin money." They work to secure additional income to provide their families with a car, home, or college educations that could not otherwise be afforded. The average woman worker is a secretary who increases family income by about 25%, and this permits many lower-middle-class families to achieve middle-class status, something the husband could not achieve for his family on his own. Sociologically as well as economically, this is an important fact: It means that women in white-collar jobs are quite often married to men who are in blue-collar jobs. The effect of this status differential within the family should not be overlooked. It helps to explain why many men oppose women working. For blue-collar men, far more than white-collar men, retain strong beliefs about the "division of labor" between the sexes. A wife who works at a higher-paid job than her blue-collar husband damages his self-esteem because he feels he has failed as a breadwinner. Research shows that both partners are lower in marriage happiness if the wife works out of necessity rather than if she works by choice. In addition, it has been found that among male blue-collar workers, discontent with life is highest for those whose wives were also working. One way out of this unhappy dilemma is to work toward the elimination of sex, class, and role stereotypes which damage the self-esteem of both men and women in the working class.

Women's status as "secondary workers" is largely the result of their roles as mothers and their lower earnings. Ironically, if there were less sex bias in employment opportunities, women's income would less frequently be "the marginal income," and there would probably be greater concern about their unemployment rates, in spite of the fact that self-supporting women, female family-heads, and families dependent on the wife's earnings would be in a much less precarious position than is now the case.

In summary, it is clear women have consistently been relegated to the lower-paying, lower-status jobs in the money economy. Their actual contribution to the economy is far below what could reasonably be expected on the basis of their education, abilities, and work experience. The occupational status of women is the major symptom of an opportunity structure that is much more limiting for women than for men. And, work in the home is not considered to be "real work" by society.

How can these situations be remedied? Equal employment opportunity legislation may be of significance, especially when it involves affirmative action programs that require employers to take the initiative in recruiting and promoting women in all types of work, prohibit sex segregating ads, and concentrate on eliminating discriminatory patterns and practices. However, additional programs must be designed to cope with institutional sexism, not just individual prejudice. Many of our present laws and court procedures help protect women against overt acts of exclusion, but they are of little use in eliminating customary patterns of behavior and cultural stereotypes that limit opportunities for all but the most aggressive of a discriminated-against group.

A serious concern over the job satisfaction of women workers indicates the need: (1) to change the cultural stereotypes about the character of females, (2) to achieve mobility and earnings parity between the sexes, (3) to substantially advance the opportunities for voluntary participation of women in the labor force, (4) to eliminate traditional factors that denigrate women who work by choice in the money economy without building new pressures that denigrate women who freely choose work in the home, and (5) to redesign the jobs of women and men to make them more intrinsically rewarding.

The Economics of Women's Liberation

by Joan Jordan

The woman question, like the black question, is dual and complex. On one side of the duality is direct economic exploitation. On the other are the myriad social forms of discrimination and exploitation, such as those that keep women from having seats in postgraduate schools or those in southern states that put the flower of southern womanhood on pedestals so high that they are not permitted to serve on juries since they are "incompetent because of sex."

Economic categories come first. In April 1968, 28.7 million American women 16 years old and over were employed outside the home. The percentage of women at work — 48 — has surpassed the peak of 36 per cent in the war year of 1945. Today, however, the vast majority of working women are married, and the age level has shifted upward to a 40-year-old median, with 53 per cent of the women between 45 and 54 at work. Almost half (49 per cent) of the women who are married, living with their husbands and have children over 6 are working. One out of every ten families has a female head, and one-fourth of all black families has a female head. About two-fifths (39 per cent) of the women who headed families classified as poor in 1966 were in the paid labor force.

Black women workers are the lowest-paid group, followed by white women, black men and white men in ascending order. However, in some categories determined by educational attainment or selected occupation, this order shifts. For instance, median income for white women in two categories —

Reprinted with permission from *New Generation*. Copyright © 1969 by the National Committee on Employment of Youth.

those with some college and those with four or more years of college — is lower than black women in those two categories, but both groups earn less than white men with one to three years of high school. In 1967 black women were also making more than white women in professional, managerial, clerical and sales occupations in the central city. This suggests that the greater self-assertiveness, independence and militancy of black women is of value and may be a causal factor in their being considered worth more.

One group of women workers seldom included in Labor Department statistics are those who do housework, child bearing and child rearing. Although some of these workers are within the market economy, most are not. Their unpaid but socially necessary labor is somewhat similar to that of unpaid serfs or peasants in relation to a growing industrializing market economy. The precapitalist formation of the family unit is necessary to the capitalist system in order to provide cheap labor power through the unpaid labor of women in the home. If women were paid equally with men, it would mean a vast redivision of the wealth.

In most cases, housework is the most unproductive work a woman can do. It is arduous, repetitive and monotonous, and its exceptionally petty nature does not provide anything that could promote the development of the woman in any way. According to a monograph by Juliet Mitchell, "Women, the Longest Revolution" (1966), it was found that in Sweden women spend 2,340 million hours a year in housework, compared with 1,290 million hours in industry. The Chase Manhattan Bank has estimated that a woman's overall working hours in the home average 99.6 per week.

As millions of women have entered the labor market, they have been pushed into the lowest-paying job categories. The median income of women compared to men has dropped from 59 per cent in 1939 to 30 per cent today. In almost every industry and occupation women are paid less than men for doing the same job. Women are massed in the lower-paying major occupations; women are passed over for on-the-job training and upgrading; women are denied advancement. Why? What excuses are given for this discrimination?

Many rationalizations are given for paying women less and keeping them from advancing. Some claim that differences in the performance of men and women on the job justify the differentials. Women, they say, are not as well prepared for jobs as men. They don't have the equivalent formal education and specific training. In addition, women don't make good supervisors; women cost the employer more in fringe benefits; women have a higher turnover rate and more absenteeism than men. Woman's place is in the home. Only once in a great while will an employer admit that it's *cheaper* to discriminate.

The case for discrimination against women because of inadequate preparation — with the implication that they lack the ambition to get the preparation — is remarkably similar to that given to justify the treatment of black workers. The vicious circle begins with the refusal of the employer to hire or promote blacks because they aren't "qualified"; continues because discrimination on these grounds intensifies discrimination on other, more prejudiced grounds; and is completed when the Negro is disinclined to get more preparation because he knows he will be discriminated against even with adequate preparation; hence he is unprepared to seize opportunities if they do open up. Women are also caught in this never-ending cycle.

In addition, the case for discriminating against women because of their lack of education has not been proved. In fact, the evidence shows that, except on the highest levels, women as a whole enter the labor market with more training and education than do men. In 1959 women had completed a median of 12.2 years of schooling compared with 11.7 years for men. Thirty-eight per cent of the women workers and only 27 per cent of the male workers had completed high school.

Consider this in light of Betty Friedan's argument that women need more education to break out of the trap of the "feminine mystique." If more education would expose the political and economic causes of the mystique, she might be right, but the realities are that even as women are becoming more and more educated, the proportion of professional women is shrinking. And even though more and more women are entering the labor force, they are being restricted to the lower-paying jobs and prevented from advancing.

There is obviously little incentive for a woman to better her skills if better positions are closed to her. In the unions, apprentice-training programs are generally restricted to white males with the rationalization that, after all, a man has a family to take care of. That this argument is used against women who are heads of families seems to bother no one.

Another rationalization for not promoting women is that they don't make good supervisors, or that both women and men prefer to work under men. This is a subjective judgment that has not been demonstrated and is subject to speculation. It may not be that women do not or could not supervise well but rather that men in management (and in unions, too — perhaps even more) fear that women will succeed too well. The relevant factor here might be the danger to the male ego. Only a man with a strong, stable core of self can see a woman as an equal human being and not feel a threat to his masculinity.

Arguments are also raised about fringe benefits. Employers claim that women cost them more in benefits than men do and on that basis justify their use of women as part-time or temporary full-time workers to avoid giving them such benefits. Their main complaint is that pregnant women are required by law to interrupt their work for a number of months, and in most union contracts the job must be held open and benefits paid by the employer. In reality, however, most union health plans exclude maternity benefits with such rationalizations as "maternity is not sickness but an act of God."

The results of several studies reported in a Labor Department Women's Bureau pamphlet ("Maternity Benefits Provisions for Employed Women") reveal that no more than 4 per cent of employed women in any one year will become pregnant. This compares with injury rates among workers at about 3 per cent in 1958, not including sickness. The benefits for pregnancy negotiated in union contracts usually are no higher than the benefits paid for sickness and disability to all workers covered by a particular contract, and total amounts of workers' compensation for injuries are increasing.

By cooperating with employers in their refusal to pay fringe benefits to women workers, male unionists are in a weak tactical position when employers try to avoid paying fringe benefits to men. Plants move to states with "right-to-work" laws or to nonunionized regions, or they just switch job classification from men's to women's work or from permanent to temporary to take advantage of discriminatory practices, thus turning the lower wage scale into a weapon to be used against male workers too.

The rationalization that turnover rates and absenteeism are higher for women than men usually ignores the fact that women generally work in the worst conditions. The turnover problem also appears to be directly related to the kind and level of work involved. The Women's Bureau of the Labor Department, in a 1950 study titled "Women in Higher Level Positions," showed that different firms gave different opinions on turnover rates. Almost all firms whose training programs were closed to women gave lack of permanency as the reason. On the other hand, several company representatives in different fields maintained that although lack of permanency generally was a deterrent to women's advancement, it was not important as far as the higher-level positions were concerned. One large department store had in fact found that there was less turnover among women in its promotional department than men.

There is at present no information on the relative rates of absenteeism of men and women, but one can assume that adequate day-care facilities for children of working mothers would be an important factor. When such facilities were established during World War II, employers testified that they greatly helped to reduce absenteeism and turnover in their plants.

Another rationalization for discriminating against women acts directly to divide the labor movement and pit one section against the other. This is what happens when employers tell skilled male workers, officers or negotiating committees that "we could give you a much higher wage if you just didn't have to drag those unskilled workers along with you." The Teamsters Council of New York City published an analysis of marginal workers in New York City, including those in the International Ladies Garment Workers Union, that indicated that women were restricted to the lower-paying jobs controlled by the union. In collusion with the employers, skilled workers would trade off better wages and working conditions of the more numerous unskilled women workers in exchange for greater gains for themselves.

To pull off this kind of a deal it is necessary to intimidate the general workers and nullify any real grievance procedures in their departments. This is done by emphasizing the "role of the woman" and the "male breadwinner" ideologies in order to create an attitude of passive "feminine" acceptance.

The old saw that a woman's place is in the home is used as a rationalization by many employers for paying lower wages and providing worse working conditions for women than men. If these employers really meant what they said, they would not hire women at all, but leave them in the home. Instead they use the feminine mystique to keep women in their place — their place being the reserve labor force.

It is interesting to follow the propaganda used to control women. During World War II idle hands were tools of the devil, Rosie the Riveter was portrayed as a dynamic, patriotic heroine and articles appeared on the advantages of bottle feeding compared to breast feeding. Immediately following World War II women at work were accused of creating juvenile delinquents at home and of competing with men, and surveys showed that eight out of ten infants who died of stomach ailments within the first year of birth were bottle-fed.

However, employers found that the rate of exploitation of men was not so profitable as that of women, so women were allowed to stay in industry — in their place. The middle-class concepts of femininity and its pseudo-psychological twin of passivity are extremely valuable to employers. In addition to providing rationales for discrimination and exploitation, they also serve to give women guilt complexes, making it easier to manipulate them. Women will often compensate by trying to work harder and for less pay. They may do the work of the executive or supervisor without the title or the salary. After all, they don't want to be dominating, aggressive, pushy or *masculine*.

The problems of "human relations in industry" are set up by industrial psychologists employed by the company, and are seen as primarily due to misunderstanding and lack of open communication. The call for more "cooperation" usually means obedience accompanied by talk.

Betty Friedan and other writers have very adequately dealt with the economic value to business of the feminine mystique, particularly in getting women to fulfill their roles as consumers and purchasers of endless commodities. Less has been said about the economic value to business of the mystique in relation to woman as the employee, as the producer of commodities.

It is naive to believe that women can be fully liberated in an economic system where profit alone — even when it means the waste of the labor power of millions of human beings and millions of working hours — is the chief determinant. It is essential, in solving women's problems, to change society. Women can and will play a key role in this general historical task, but they cannot expect to solve their problems without a struggle. Equality will not be given them as a gift. It must be fought for and won as a human right.

Nevertheless, it is not sufficient to equate the woman question with the struggle of the deprived classes generally. One can no more say to women than to blacks, "Join us and when we have socialism your needs will be met." Because the woman question is a dual problem, because women suffer special forms of discrimination and exploitation in addition to being workers, there is a need for special organizations and special demands to meet their needs.

Economic organization is a necessity, but most unions have either defaulted in relation to organizing women or used them to protect skilled workers' jobs or as the expendable element in contract negotiations. Although one-third of the present labor force is composed of women, only 15 per cent of them are organized into unions.

The current ferment among women may, however, change that. Union leaders know a good thing when they see it. In 1961 and 1962 three-fourths of all new members organized in California were women, and this was in spite of the fact that there was a drop in overall union membership in the state at that time. These women came from both government and private jobs. Given the chauvinistic male exploitative attitudes of many union men as well as employers toward women, it is obvious, however, that other organizations are needed too.

Two groups may be of particular interest: the Women's Bureau of the United Auto Workers, and the Negro American Labor Council. The Women's Bureau was organized in 1953, when automation hit Detroit, and women, some with as much as fifteen years' seniority, were laid off. They organized and went to the UAW convention with demands to be included not only in the constitution but in contract demands as well. The critical demand was concerned with job security and promotion in a shrinking labor market. The goal was to prevent women from being used as a reserve labor force and driven back to the home during periods of economic contraction.

The Negro American Labor Council was developed in the late 1950's as an organization of black trade unionists fighting to get into unions, to receive apprentice training, upgrading and promotion on the job, and to run candidates for union office and policy-making bodies. Such an organization as this, based on sex instead of color, would seem feasible for women. NALC members come from many unions and exist independently of any one union. In contrast, the Women's Bureau is within one union.

Special economic demands must be made. Three main trends of sexual discrimination have become more and more common in this decade. The first is to lay off women and rehire men in women's classifications at women's wages, and was used in the 1953 recession in Detroit. However, the men challenged this tactic; there was no feminine mystique to keep *them* passive.

The second trend is to lay off men and use more women in jobs that have been reclassified from men's to women's, at lower wages. For instance, electrical assembly in California used to be men's work, but for years the men in the union felt they could do better and should get more than women. As the gap in wages and conditions widened, so did the difference between the number of men and women in the union and also the number of nonunion women in industry. In both cases the numbers of women relative to men increased as their wages relative to men's decreased. Electrical-assembly and electronics industries grew rapidly during and after the war. By that time the work had become known as women's work "traditionally," and new employees were recruited from among women. The men in the union complained bitterly about how the women's wages kept theirs down because women worked so cheaply and were taking all the jobs, yet this was a result of their original position that they should get more than women.

Naked self-interest should have led the women to 1) organize a women's caucus; 2) raise their demands, with priority on job security through many methods, but especially through the sliding scale of hours such as the thirty-hour week at forty-hour pay; and 3) develop tactics that would convince their union brothers of the necessity of supporting them, neutralize those they couldn't convince and actively fight those in open opposition.

The Civil Rights Bill of 1964 supposedly banned discrimination based on sex. However, the law is simply ignored by many corporations. They claim, as did Fibreboard of California recently, that they are "caught" between the federal law and the state protective laws in such areas as hours, lifting and overtime penalty pay. In reality they are using the protective laws to maintain discrimination and at the same time following a strategy designed to smash these laws. Then in a contracting labor market (i.e., with many idle workers eager to get jobs at any salary) they could extend the working day to ten or twelve hours or more without overtime pay or the right to refuse. . . .

The third trend of economic exploitation is to use more part-time workers and full-time temporary workers to avoid paying fringe benefits. This can be overcome by demands for equal pay to workers of this type, and complete medical coverage beginning immediately and based on the length of time in industry rather than with a given employer; pro-rated vacations and the scheduling of work over the year to keep on a full-time regular crew; and holiday pay no matter when the worker joined the company.

Social demands are important, too, of course, and must be made along with demands for economic reform, because economic reforms alone will not solve all the problems facing both men and women in contemporary American society. Some of the most pressing are:

— Free public nurseries and child-care centers for all working mothers.
— Planned-parenthood centers available to any man or woman.
— Legal abortions in free, well-staffed clinics.
— Summer camps for all children.
— Reorganization of home chores by application of mass-production methods.
— Equal economic, social and intellectual opportunities.
— Fathers and mothers on four-hour days or shortened work weeks so that fathers may regain their lost role and share in the growth experiences of their children, as suggested by Ashley Montagu.
— Payment of maternity and paternity leaves for three to five years while parents work two, four or at most six hours daily in child-care centers and nurseries with their children and also attend classes on child development with specialists.
— Payment of wages to mothers for bearing and raising children.

This last reform would give social recognition and remuneration for the "job" of motherhood, making it as important as any other form of labor. It would eliminate both victimization due to biological necessity and marriages based on economic necessity. It would recognize that having children is a part of the socially necessary labor in the reproduction of life. It would help to eliminate "commodity" relations between people and establish relations based on personality and emotional needs instead. It would produce strong, self-confident men and women who did not suffer from the sicknesses and neuroses of exploitative relations. Men and women could then see each other as equal human beings with unequal development of potentialities — as persons instead of things.

White Working-Class Youth

by R. J. Krickus

Contrary to what the news media, academics, and the "cosmopolitan" Left imply, the average American youngster is not doing his thing on a university campus. By 1985, it is estimated, only 14 percent of America's population will be graduates of four-year colleges. The Bureau of Labor Statistics reports that, in 1968, 65.4 percent of our high school graduates sought employment upon graduating and did not enter college. We are talking about the single largest proportion of our youth, yet in-depth studies of their psychological, social, economic, and political problems are hardly available.

Given the Republicans' campaign to wrest working-class votes from the Democrats and the latter's natural inclination to stave off a GOP raid, one would think that adroit operatives in both parties would be uncovering relevant data about this sought-after target. That's not so. Staff people, speech-writers, and researchers in Washington remain in an appalling state of ignorance about working-class youth. I know of a "youth agency" in Health, Education and Welfare that has a three-fold classification of youth in the United States — "black," "Mexican-American," and "college student." Last summer an Office of Education analyst told me that he had nearly completed a study of our nation's educational priorities before realizing he had overlooked the needs of white noncollege youth.

Academia has been turned on by the "counter culture" and campus unrest, but it pays little attention to the life-style of the young factory worker, the political socialization of his

Reprinted with permission of the author and *Dissent* Magazine. Copyright © 1971 by *Dissent*.

co-workers, and the plight of his wife. It is often assumed that these young people have become melded into the American middle class. This is a somewhat generous explanation, since there is convincing evidence that many academics who pander to the fashionable just do not think working-class youth are worthwhile research material.

The mass media's treatment of young workers also reflects the tunnel vision of middle-class America. Coverage is intermittent at best, usually superficial, and always manifests a parochial (class) bias. The truck driver, supermarket clerk, and steel worker's wife are rarely the subject matter of TV documentaries, much less of TV drama. How many movies has Hollywood produced in the last ten years that sympathetically treat the frustrations of working Americans? There is, of course, *Joe,* an abomination that deserves mention only because many otherwise thoughtful people on the Left believe that the stereotyped Joe Curran fairly represents what the American workingman would be like if his "natural instincts" ever rose to the surface of his consciousness. On the rare occasions when working-class youths receive attention (usually as a by-product of investigation into the problems of affluent youngsters), they are depicted as racist, superhawk cultural yahoos. Yet the young men and women who are portrayed in such one-dimensional terms must grapple with the same kinds of problems — "who am I," "how should I spend my life," "is my work meaningful" — which produce alienation among campus youth.

II

In one of the few recent studies of working-class youth, William Simon and John Gagnon write:

> When compared to the most conservative and minimal goals set for contemporary education—except perhaps the dubious goal of insuring reasonably conformist behavior—schools in the working-class areas can only be described as undramatic disaster areas.

Journalist-teacher Peter Binzen in his *White Town U.S.A.* found that the performance of his white students in the Kensington area of Philadelphia approached that of black ghetto children. Binzen's findings will not shock even the casual observer of working-class communities where inferior teachers and inadequate facilities characterize the educational system.

Vocational schools often are mere holding areas for problem students. They rarely provide instruction that is pointed to the demands of the student. College preparatory curricula are grossly inadequate. The son of a factory worker with college potential is too often shunted off to industrial school or pushed out to work. True, working-class parents do not encourage academic achievement to the extent true of middle-class families. But in many cases this restrictive outlook is less a sign of anti-intellectualism than a clear insight into the economics of higher education.

No wonder the drop-out rate in working-class school systems is alarmingly high. In the Highlandtown-Canton area of Baltimore one-third of the high school students drop out and in the Mayfield-Murray Hill district of Cleveland the figure is 50 percent. The crisis of urban education is by no means confined to nonwhite communities.

Lacking the educational perspective or experiences that broaden one's social vision, the working-class youngster, as his parents, feels threatened by the changes swirling about him. It is difficult for him to sympathize with dissident behavior.* He is inclined to condemn the activities of long-haired youth, student demonstrators, and articulate black activists who, when breaking the rules of the game, seem to receive sympathetic support from the mass media, government, and the educational system. He knows that if *he* violated the laws the college kids break, he would be arrested without much fanfare or discussion about the grievances that led to his antisocial behavior. He is not unfeeling about the plight of the poor and disadvantaged, but he was taught and he believes in the American credo that a man's success or failure

---

*A growing number of working-class kids smoke pot, wear long hair, and favor hippie-type clothes, but in many cases these kids are as straight as their parents on other matters. Simon and Gagnon found that the single largest group among the youngsters they studied were family-oriented and by and large adopted the worldview of their parents on most issues.

depends upon whether or not he is prepared to work hard for what he wants. Unfortunately, this belief deters him from adequately dealing with problems germane to his own well-being.

The alienation of many black youths has been mollified by virtue of the black community's invigorated sense of group identity. Against the backdrop of poverty and racial prejudice, this may not offer much consolation; yet the Negro who shares the workbench with a white youth feels "plugged into" the movement for social change. Like black people of all ages, he derives emotional support from the activities of leaders like Malcolm X and Martin Luther King. But the white working-class youth has no role model to help him reduce his frustration.

III

Since the end of World War II, a myth has evolved that the American worker has become entrenched in middle-class affluence. As of today, the take-home pay of the average factory hand or clerk with three dependents is slightly over $100.00 per week. In the New York/New Jersey metropolitan area, the Department of Labor states that $11,236 is needed to maintain a moderate level of living for a family of this size. But as of 1967, 61.7 percent of the white families living in New York City earned $9,000 per year or less. Consumer prices are rising faster than wages. Consequently, the take-home pay of the average salaried worker, in terms of purchasing power, was less in 1969 than it had been in 1968.

The prospects of the young drop-out (600,000 American youngsters drop out of high school every year) and the recent high school graduate may be even more dismal today than a decade ago. Lacking a job record or proper vocational training, young workers encounter serious employment difficulties. This age group is growing in absolute numbers at a time when the supply of jobs for which unskilled youth can qualify is declining.

In the past, workers could feel some security from the knowledge that a more stable or higher paying position was within reach if one stuck it out. But in the 1970s most workers cannot anticipate moving up the job ladder in this fashion. A study of production workers by the Survey Research Center of the University of Michigan disclosed that two-thirds of the respondents believed they had no prospect of advancing beyond their present jobs.

The Rosow Report documents that at the outset of his work history, the young worker may earn a relatively good salary. But marriage and growing family responsibilities gradually erode his income, and his salary fails to keep pace with his expenditures. Lacking seniority, he is likely to be laid off during economic slowdowns, and this threat has prompted many young workers to leave better-paying positions in industry for municipal jobs as policemen or firemen, which pay less but offer more job security.

Over the long pull, a secure job may be less important than the disappearance of work options that can engender a sense of accomplishment in one's work. A growing number of young workers are dissatisfied with their jobs. Late bloomers who find themselves trapped in dead-end jobs are rarely given a second chance. This may account for the rising incidence of drug abuse in factories, high rates of turn-over, and mounting absenteeism.

Judson Gooding writes that tedious and repetitious jobs have provoked auto workers to sabotage the assembly line. Such outbursts of frustration are not new. Fourteen years ago I worked the "graveyard shift" in a can factory. It was a common practice several times an evening to shut down the endless flow of beer cans. The process was foolproof and simple. A crumpled can or one turned in the wrong direction would ultimately foul up the system. This afforded us a rest. But a respite from our monotonous work was secondary to the keen pleasure we derived from the thought that the boss knew what we were doing, but could not do anything about our protest. Try though I did, I could not induce my co-workers to relate their dissatisfaction to the corporate structure or political system. My failure to get through was not unanticipated, for in my neighborhood (the Clinton Hill area of Newark) socioeconomic problems were deemed a function of one's personal inability to cope, and not as manifestations of a larger social problem.

Today job dissatisfaction is prevalent among workers who have been reared in an era of prosperity and are but dimly aware of the depression. Approximately 21 million Americans between the ages of 15 and 29 are out of school and never graduated from a college. In many industries they are the backbone of the rank and file. Approximately 40 percent of the auto workers are under 35 and in some auto plants 70 percent of the production-line workers are under 30.

These working-class youths comprise a subculture in which affluence is not taken for granted. In the hippie areas of our larger cities numerous free services are made available to estranged middle-class youngsters, yet one does not find these same services in working-class communities where the need is at least as great. The son of a corporation executive who is rewarded with a social disease as a consequence of a weekend fling at a crash pad can go to a free clinic and receive medical attention. Meanwhile, the young gas station attendant who may be cursed by the same affliction must shell out $10 or $15 for a penicillin shot. As usual in our economic system, the workingman subsidizes the rich and well-connected.

The young worker has been bedazzled by the allure of new automobiles and a suburban home filled with luxurious furniture and labor-saving appliances. Much like the black youth who is caught in a racial bind, he is ensnared in a socioeconomic bind. He sees no exit from a life of economic insecurity, boredom, and an income never quite providing him with the resources to acquire those things he wants.

IV

A growing number of young workers seem to be becoming politically restive. They will tell you that government, the major parties, union leadership, management, and the media are insensitive to their needs. George Wallace was the first national political figure to appreciate the depth of their despair and he provided them with a way of mobilizing their discontent and channeling it politically. While most white workers rejected Wallace, his appeal to them was a symptom of their estrangement from our mainstream institutions. Outside the South his movement was nourished primarily by young white workers.

In the cities and suburbs where the young workers live, they have good reason to be cynical about government. Owners of modest homes pay a disproportionate share of the taxes, yet their streets, schools, and recreational facilities are in a state of disrepair. Corruption is highly visible, the streets are unsafe, and there is a feeling that "their own" politicians are selling them out. A declining faith in government prevails in the "reformed" cities as well, for as James Q. Wilson has observed, many big city mayors seem more concerned about foundations, urban consultants, and agency chiefs in Washington than about the complaints of their constituents. Many young workers are both resentful of Washington's neglect and fearful of programs they deem prejudicial to their communities.

Lewis Carliner, in a recent workshop devoted to the problems of young workers, found they are concerned about their "civil rights" at work — unfair disciplinary procedures, shift assignments, and overtime duty. They are cynical about management's pronouncements regarding the "public interest," since they often work in filthy surroundings under unsafe conditions.* At the same time, they are impatient with their union leaders and the older workers. They want a greater say in decisions affecting life in the plant. Unlike their fathers, promises about future benefits do not silence them. This rising militancy explains wildcat strikes not sanctioned by union officials (work stoppages jumped by 50 percent in the period 1965-1970), dissident caucuses within the union movement, and attempts to break away from present unions altogether.

---

*A presidential commission was formed to study unrest on college campuses after students were tragically killed at Kent State and Jackson State. Some 14,000 workers are killed in industrial accidents every year, yet concerned citizens have not expressed alarm about this appalling statistic.

Nor should we overlook the problems that confront the young workingman in his community. I have traveled widely throughout the urban North in the last year. On my visits to working-class communities, I have found neighborhood organizations springing up where none had existed before. In North Newark, Southeast Baltimore, and Lake County, Indiana, to cite a few examples, working-class whites are forming community organizations as progressive alternatives to right-wing demagogues who have been attempting to exploit the white communities' alienation.*

A final word of caution. The most articulate members of the liberal and radical Left often live in a cosmopolitan subculture that is alien to the average workingman. This cultural chasm accounts in part for past neglect of the working class and forms a roadblock to a firm political coalition with lower-middle-class whites. In these circles one still hears talk about crypto-fascists controlling the construction unions and Nazis in hard hats running amok on the streets assaulting students. The implication that all construction workers are bent on suppressing dissent through violence and the tendency to label the workingman a "hard hat" is fashionable in liberal and radical circles alike.**

Many working-class Americans believe that revolutionary

---

*Having recognized the need for community organization, a caveat is in order. Proponents of community development have made exaggerated claims about citizen power and participation. Working-class whites are in desperate need of neighborhood structures to mobilize power but many, if not most, of our pressing domestic problems — housing, education, employment, medical care, etc.—require a national thrust to extract massive assistance from Washington. This means the construction of a new political coalition of blacks, working-class whites, liberals, students, and Democratic radicals. While it is fashionable to debunk coalitions that smack of the New Deal, a coalition of this kind is the only feasible road to democratic change in the United States in the 1970s.

**An example of activists' defining the workingman's problems through a middle-class prism occurred last year in Gary, Indiana. Young environmentalists had decided that pollution was an issue that would spark the interests of workers in that grimy industrial city. Their antipollution campaign, however, prompted the workers to respond with a slogan of their own: "Pollution — love it or leave it." Reassessing their position, the environmentalists gained the interest of the workers when they zeroed in on conditions in the factories — oil-strew floors, leaking gas, smoke emissions, and so on.

elitists are exploiting their privileged position to side-step the rules by which "straights" must abide. Those who apologize for the excesses of the student revolutionaries and the Panthers contribute to the stereotypes by which workers see radicals as subversives and liberals as hostile to the working-class American. The double standard that treats the alienation of middle-class youth sympathetically and denies the plight of the young worker promotes such stereotyping.

We are asked to understand college dissidents, to sympathize with their problems, and to make an effort to communicate with them. We should. But the same kind of compassion and indulgence must be directed at the bulk of our noncollege youngsters, for they too have legitimate problems. We cannot hope to eliminate poverty, racism, urban blight, and defense spending beyond our security requirements unless we gain rapport with those youngsters who drive trucks, clerk in department stores, and pump gas.

The Young Worker –
Challenging the Work Ethic?

from *Work in America*

More than any other group, it appears that young people
have taken the lead in demanding better working conditions.
Out of a workforce of more than 85 million, 22½ million are
under the age of 30. As noted earlier, these young workers are
more affluent and better educated than their parents were
at their age. Factually, that is nearly all that can be gen-
eralized about this group. But it is asserted by such authors
as Kenneth Keniston, Theodore Roszak, Charles Reich, and
others, that great numbers of young people in this age group
are members of a counter-culture. The President's Commission on Campus Unrest wrote that this subculture "found its
identity in a rejection of the work ethic, materialism, and
conventional social norms and pieties." Many writers have
stressed the alleged revolt against work, "a new 'anti-work
ethic' . . . a new, deep-seated rejection by the young of the traditional American faith in hard work." But empirical findings
do not always support the impressionistic commentaries.

It is commonly agreed that there is a difference between
the in-mode behavior of youth and their real attitudes. Many
young people do wear beads, listen to rock music, and occasionally smoke pot, but few actually live in communes (and
these few may be working very hard), and even fewer are so
alienated that they are unwilling to play a productive role
in society. Daniel Yankelovich conducted national attitude
studies of college students from 1968 to 1971 and found that
two-thirds of college students profess mainstream views in

Reprinted from *Work in America*, Report of a Special Task Force to the
Secretary of Health, Education, and Welfare; The MIT Press, 1973.

general. But their feelings in particular about work (and private business) are even more affirmative:

— 79% believe that commitment to a meaningful career is a very important part of a person's life.
— 85% feel business is entitled to make a profit.
— 75% believe it is morally wrong to collect welfare when you can work.
— Only 30% would welcome less emphasis on working hard.

While student feelings about work itself are generally high, Yankelovich found that attitudes towards authority are changing rapidly. In 1968 over half (56%) of all students indicated that they did not mind the future prospect of being "bossed around" on the job. By 1971 only one out of three students (36%) saw themselves willingly submitting to such authority. Equally important, while 86% of these students still believe that society needs some legally based authority to prevent chaos, they nevertheless see a distinction between this necessity and an authoritarian work setting.

Yankelovich also found a shift in student opinion on the issue that "hard work will always pay off" from a 69% affirmation in 1968 to a 39% affirmation in 1971. This certainly was, in part, indicative of the conditions in the job market for college graduates in 1971. But more basically, we believe, it highlights a paradox inherent in a populace with increasing educational achievement. Along with the mass media, education and its credentials are raising expectations faster than the economic system can meet them. Much of what is interpreted as anti-work attitudes on the part of youth, then, may be their appraisal of the kinds of jobs that are open to them.

The following case study of a young woman who is a recent college graduate illustrates the gap between expectations and reality:

I didn't go to school for four years to type. I'm bored; continuously humiliated. They sent me to Xerox school for three hours. ... I realize that I sound cocky, but after you've been in the academic world, after you've had your own class (as a **student** teacher) and made your own plans, and someone tries to teach you to push a button—you get pretty mad. They even gave me a goldplated plaque to show I've learned how to use the machine.

The problem is compounded by the number of students who are leaving school with advanced degrees, like the young Chicago lawyer in the following case:

> You can't wait to get out and get a job that will let you do something that's really important.... You think you're one of the elite. Then you go to a place like the Loop and there are all these lawyers, accountants, etc., and you realize that you're just a lawyer. No, not even a lawyer—an employee; you have to check in at nine and leave at five. I had lots of those jobs— summers—where you punch in and punch out. You think it's going to be different but it isn't. You're in the rut like everybody else.

Today's youth are expecting a great deal of intrinsic reward from work. Yankelovich found that students rank the opportunity to "make a contribution," "job challenge," and the chance to find "self-expression" at the top of the list of influences on their career choice. A 1960 survey of over 400,000 high school students was repeated for a representative sample in 1970, and the findings showed a marked shift from the students valuing job security and opportunity for promotion in 1960 to valuing "freedom to make my own decisions" and "work that seems important to me" in 1970.

Many of these student findings were replicated in the University of Michigan Survey of Working Conditions sample of young workers. For example, it seems as true of young workers as it is of students that they expect a great deal of fulfillment from work. But the Survey findings show that young workers are not deriving a great deal of satisfaction from the work they are doing. Less than a quarter of young workers reply "very often" when asked the question, "How often do you feel you leave work with a good feeling that you have done something particularly well?"

Age Group	Percentage Answering "Very Often"
Under 20	23
21-29	25
30-44	38
45-64	43
65 and over	53

Other findings document that young workers place more importance on the value of interesting work and their ability to grow on the job than do their elders. They also place less importance than do older workers on such extrinsic factors as security and whether or not they are asked to do excessive amounts of work. But the Survey documents a significant gap between the expectations or values of the young workers and what they actually experience on the job. Young workers rate their jobs lower than do older workers on how well their jobs actually live up to the factors they most sought in work. For example, the young value challenging work highly but say that the work they are doing has a low level of challenge.

It has also been found that a much higher percentage of younger than older workers feel that management emphasizes the *quantity* more than the *quality* of their work. Furthermore, it is shown that this adversely affects the satisfaction of younger workers. Such findings contradict the viewpoint that there is a weakening of the "moral fiber" of youth. . . .

In summary, we interpret these various findings not as demonstrating a shift away from valuing work *per se* among young people, but as a shift away from their willingness to take on meaningless work in an authoritarian setting that offers only extrinsic rewards. We agree with Willis Harman that:

> The shape of the future will no more be patterned after the hippie movement and the Youth Revolution than the Industrial Age could have been inferred from the "New Age" values of the Anabaptists.

A mistake is made, however, if one believes that the new attitudes toward authority and the meaning of work are limited to hippies. Judson Gooding writes that young managers, both graduates of business schools and executive trainees, "reflect the passionate concerns of youth in the 1970's — for individuality, openness, humanism, concern and change — and they are determined to be heard."

Some young people are rejecting the corporate or bureaucratic worlds, while not rejecting work or the concept of work or profit. Gooding tells of one young former executive who quit his job with a major corporation because

> you felt like a small cog. Working there was dehumanizing and the struggle to get to the top didn't seem worth it. They made no effort to encourage your participation. The decisions were made in those rooms with closed doors. . . . The serious error they made with me was not giving me a glimpse of the big picture from time to time, so I could go back to my little detail, understanding how it related to the whole.

This young man has now organized his own small business and designed his own job. As the publisher of a counterculture newspaper, he might be considered a radical in his beliefs and life style, yet he says "profit is not an evil." Of course, many young workers do question the *use* of profits, especially those profits that they feel are made at the expense of society or the environment. Some businesses themselves are adopting this same attitude.

It may be useful to analyze the views of today's youth not in terms of their parents' values but in terms of the beliefs of their grandparents. Today's youth believe in independence, freedom, and risk — in short, they may have the entrepreneurial spirit of early capitalism. Certainly they are more attracted to small and growing companies, to small businesses and to handicrafts, than to the bureaucracy, be it privately or publicly owned. (The declining opportunity for such small-scale endeavors probably contributes to both the job dissatisfaction of the young and their apparent lack of commitment to the kinds of jobs that are available.) On the other hand, their parents share a managerial ethic that reflects the need for security, order, and dependence that is born of hard times. Of course, this is being a bit unfair to the older generation and a bit over-generous with our youth, but it serves to get us away from the simplistic thinking that the "Protestant ethic has been abandoned." Who in America ever had the Protestant ethic and when? Did we have it in the thirties? Did the poor people or even middle-class people ever have it? It is argued by Sebastian deGrazia that the Protestant ethic was never more than a myth engendered by the owner and managerial classes to motivate the lower working class — a myth which the latter never fully accepted. Clearly, it is difficult to measure the past allegiance of a populace to an ideology.

But we *can* measure the impact of the present work environment on youth's motivation to work. For example, the Survey of Working Conditions found that youth seem to have a lower attachment to work than their elders on the same job. There are several reasons other than a change in the work ethic why this might be so. *First,* as we have already posited, young people have high expectations generated by their greater education. *Second,* their greater affluence makes them less tolerant of unrewarding jobs. *Third,* many new workers, particularly women, are voluntary workers. They are more demanding because they don't *have* to take a job. *Fourth,* all authority in our society is being challenged — professional athletes challenge owners, journalists challenge editors, consumers challenge manufacturers, the moral authority of religion, nation, and elders is challenged. *Fifth,* many former students are demanding what they achieved in part on their campuses a few years ago — a voice in setting the goals of the organization. The lecture has been *passé* for several years on many campuses — in colloquia and in seminars students challenge teachers. Managers are now facing the products of this progressive education. (One wonders what will happen when the children of today's open classroom, who have been taught to set their own goals and plan their own schedules, enter the workforce.) *Sixth,* young blue-collar workers, who have grown up in an environment in which equality is called for in all institutions, are demanding the same rights and expressing the same values as university graduates. *Seventh,* there is growing professionalism among many young white-collar workers. They now have loyalty to their peer group or to their task or discipline, where once they had loyalty to their work organization.

In sum, it does not appear that young workers have a lower commitment to work than their elders. The problem lies in the interaction between work itself and the changing social character of today's generation, and in the failure of decision makers in business, labor, and government to recognize this fact.

The young worker is in revolt not against work but against the authoritarian system developed by industrial engineers who felt that "the worker was stupid, overly emotional . . . insecure and afraid of responsibility." This viewpoint is summed up in Frederick Taylor's classic dictum to the worker:

> For success, then, let me give one simple piece of advice beyond all others. Every day, year in and year out, each man should ask himself, over and over again, two questions. First, "What is the name of the man I am now working for?" and having answered this definitely, then, "What does this man want me to do, right now?"

The simplistic authoritarianism in this statement would appear ludicrous to the young worker who is not the uneducated and irresponsible person on whom Taylor's system was premised. Yet, many in industry continue to support a system of motivation that was created in an era when people were willing to be motivated by the stick. As an alternative to this approach, many personnel managers have offered the carrot as a motivator, only to find that young people also fail to respond to this approach.

From our reading of what youth wants, it appears that under current policies, employers may not be able to motivate young workers at all. Instead, employers must create conditions in which the worker can motivate himself. This concept is not as strange as it seems. From biographies of artists, athletes, and successful businessmen, one finds invariably that these people set goals for themselves. The most rewarding race is probably one that one runs against oneself. Young people seem to realize this, They talk less positively than do their elders about competition with others. But they do talk about self-actualization and other "private" values. Yankelovich found that 40% of students — an increasing percentage — do not believe that "competition encourages excellence," and 80% would welcome more emphasis in the society on self-expression.

Compared to previous generations, the young person of today wants to measure his improvement against a standard he sets for himself. (Clearly, there is much more inner-direction than David Riesman would have predicted two decades ago.) The problem with the way work is organized today is that it will not allow the worker to realize his own goals. Because of the legacy of Taylorism, organizations set a fixed standard for the worker, but they often do not tell him clearly why that standard was set or how it was set. More often than not, the standard is inappropriate for the worker. And, in a strange contradiction to the philosophy of efficient management, the organization seldom gives the worker the where-withal to achieve the standard. It is as if the runner did not know where the finish line was; the rules make it a race that no worker can win.

It is problematic whether the intolerance among young workers of such poor management signals temporary or enduring changes in the work ethic. More important is how management and society will reckon with the new emphasis that the workplace should lose its authoritarian aura and become a setting for satisfying and self-actualizing activity.

"They Won't Work"–The End of the Protestant Ethic and All That

by Ivar Berg

Dissimilar and divided as they have often appeared on other counts, it has been a longstanding commonplace about Americans that thrift, diligence in work, an instinct for craftsmanship, and a capacity for deferring gratification were traits they both shared and commended to the world. Such traits made us economically productive, and in being so we served our consciences no less than our pocketbooks; it is no wonder that the Protestant Ethic in America has found adherents among Catholics and Jews and Muslims no less than among Presbyterians and Lutherans. The philosophical gap in this way of life — between personal worth and market value — we early and conveniently bridged by adorning economic necessity with all the medals of moral virtue. The net effect was to impart a high order of legitimacy to an economic system whose individual members could be credited or blamed for their own circumstances according to the degree of their prosperity.

Since the system is seen as the very vehicle of moral behavior, we have tinkered with it only occasionally — through homestead laws, anti-trust statutes, selected regulatory measures, more benign collective bargaining laws, and, in recent times, provisions to broaden access to education. By these adjustments we have sought to compensate for gross inequalities at the starting lines of the competitive race. That all but a very few citizens tried to enter the race was not remarkable. Poor Richard's aphorisms about the rewards of self-

Reprinted from *The Columbia Forum*, Winter 1973, Vol. II, No. 1. Copyright © 1973 by The Trustees of Columbia University in the City of New York.

discipline, diligence, and the alert pursuit of opportunity are with us yet, in the inelegant but expressive *summa:* "You can't get something for nothing." Few contest it.

But who has not recently heard the news, in one form or another, that after nearly two hundred years Americans are renouncing the Protestant Ethic for new and spreading heresies? Decades ago a similar alarm was raised by persons who overestimated (long before Joe McCarthy and Whittaker Chambers) the allure of the European doctrines of "collectivism." In our own time, however, the news is passed among many more than that small contingent of witchhunters of other times, and troubles those never seriously worried by the radical Left. Thoughtful parents, for example, who can abide their offspring's clothes and music and coiffure — even their questioning of marriage — are troubled by their insistence on "personal authenticity," by their attraction to communal values, and by their calling into question the worth of competition, of status-seeking, and of material consumption. The impact of the so-called youth culture is threatening not because it has borrowed occasional terms of opprobrium from the orthodox Left — dependably, "people outgrow that" — but because questions are asked that have little to do with the state and ownership.

Additional evidence that stock in the Protestant Ethic is low is readily inferred by some from the behavior of the working classes. We are told, for example, that workers are more independent, less attentive to their obligations, more prone to absenteeism and generally less accepting of supervisory and managerial authority — and this despite the fact that unemployment rates have become uncommonly high. It is even more remarkable, perhaps, that absenteeism and other indicators of loose industrial discipline have allegedly risen among the hitherto well-behaved white-collar workers, whose own unemployment rates have also increased dramatically.

No one is accustomed to seeing such evidence of workers' deficiencies side by side with high unemployment statistics, and their rubbing together has produced heat. Thus one hears annoyance expressed over the fact that blacks are proportionately represented among the absentees from relatively high-paying auto factories. Surely when their own leaders deplore the blacks' unemployment rate, employed black workers should be happy with jobs and weekly paychecks; surely they ought not to tempt their employers by negligent attendance.

And when one looks at the unions, what should one make of, say, the rules requiring duplicative work in printing shops; the firemen who famously tend no fires on diesel locomotives; the work rules which prescribe the width of paint brushes, the size of crews, the number of plumbing vents to be installed in which houses by construction workers? Nor is there much sign of guilty feeling among workers over these (as Veblen dubbed them) "strategies of independence," an omission that amazes observers to whom the "withdrawal of efficiency" (as labor calls it) seems thoroughly shameful. All is insouciance and euphemism, apparently.

But beyond doubt the most inflammatory evidence offered for the end of the Ethic is the testimony of the public welfare rolls, statistics rarely mentioned in editorials, summer cottages, seminars, or corporate board-rooms without the word "scandalous" appended. Indeed, so famous are the welfare figures now that they need no rehearsal here. It suffices to say that they are favored above all other demonstrations that "people don't want to work."

The condition of the Protestant Ethic may, however, be too glibly stated. "For instance" is notoriously not proof, and not all observers will infer the same conclusions from a given statistic or set of facts. Thus it is at least possible that the Ethic is alive though not entirely well, and that a very different diagnosis can be made. That diagnosis suggests that work does occupy a central place in the lives of most Americans but that the legitimacy of "the system" — what and whom one works for — is much in doubt. Among the faithful who work in the old imperative way, this widening doubt can easily inspire resentment, for it could imply that they themselves are naive at the best, downright foolish at worst. This explains the censorious tone so often taken toward defectors, who might otherwise be seen only as deficient or self-damaging.

One could argue, first off, that the young are at least as interested in work as any generation has been at the school-leaving age. (Consider that even the so-called social drop-outs who turn to communes enter into social compacts requiring individual contributions of labor the magnitudes of which never fail to surprise the visiting journalists from the Sunday supplements.) But within the conventional labor markets and the jobs they offer, the skeptical young complain of, among other things, educational requirements that increasingly exceed what employers can actually use, a criticism which can be sustained in an extraordinarily large number and variety of work settings. The demonstrable consequence for those employed, of any age, is dissatisfaction with the work, frustration of talents, and turnover — whose statistics are more often cited as proof of a widespread indifference toward work than as signs of managerial irrationality. No one can accurately assess how much of business and industry's rates of mental illness and alcoholism begin with thwarted abilities. It should surprise no one, least of all modern employers spending vast sums on "morale" and "human relations" programs, that the dissatisfaction of underutilized workers can reflect itself in expensive personnel and production problems.

Nor is the "withdrawal of efficiency" news. Sociologists have been reporting for more than forty years, even before the pioneering studies of workers in Western Electric's Hawthorne works, that employees will "bank" work, will invent concealed time-saving improvements on their own machines, and, in general and wherever possible, seek their own ratio of monetary-to-nonmonetary satisfactions in their shops, offices, and factory lines. In other days, it was the rare top-level manager who would not, in unemotional moments, acknowledge that workers were no less rational for making the most of every comfort possible to them. That younger, bolder, and better educated workers may have elaborated the preferences of older immigrant and Depression-scarred workers should not puzzle us.

It may of course be true that workers' independence is

on the rise. But it is not necessarily clear that workers' motivations have changed from those long ago adduced in social science studies of informal groups. Many of these studies, in their 'assessments of productivity, pointed specifically to the crucial work of managers. It may well be that we overlook that work in our assertions about employees.

Take the matter of "featherbedding," about which publicists, managers, trade-association spokesmen, and others regularly remind us. The term is applied to work rules covering an enormous number of practices in innumerable work settings. The history of the most celebrated work rules, including those mentioned earlier, shows that they were formulated within the bargaining process, with employers obtaining something of great value in return for an "arrangement" managers never thought would be problematic. Railroad managers, for example, simply did not expect that diesel engines would revolutionize railroad technology, and traded a seat for firemen in these engines for a favorable wage settlement. The seat could of course be brought back in a reversal of the bargain: workers, no less than management, conform to that article of our creed which encourages us to husband our capital, whatever it might be.

The responsibility for non-work can be similarly redistributed in other industries. Plumbing vents, for example, are typically required by building codes, whose terms most often reflect, not the sinful "make-work" instincts of construction workers acting unilaterally, but the effectiveness and ethics of municipal governments, contractors, and supporting union officials. Indeed, in much recent muttering about the devaluation of work, one might suppose that management had nothing to *do* with work.

Even the shockingly large number of people receiving welfare payments — solely or in addition to wages — can be seen in more than one light. Those persons who suppose that the welfare increases in the nation's largest cities provide statistical indices of the Ethic's demise must confront some inconvenient facts. For example, among heads of families who work full-time, about 7 percent earn an income at what has come to be called the poverty level. Among persons who are fully employed but without spouses or family, fully 30 percent are impoverished. "In fact," wrote two sociologists recently, "about a third of all impoverished families (2.4 million in 1967) are headed by a fully employed person. Another million 'unrelated individuals' are in the same situation — fully employed but poor. Millions more live at the margins of poverty." These multi-millions may have something to tell us about the state of work in America. At the very least, they are Protestant Ethic Loyalists like none that we have imagined — or lately heard from.

If a sizable number of actual welfare recipients are fully employed, another sizable number are under-employed; and a very significant number of eligible under-employed, unemployed, and impoverished workers are not beneficiaries of welfare at all. A survey of low-income families in Detroit in 1965, for example, shows that 43 percent of eligible recipients in that city were not on the welfare rolls. In New York City in 1968, approximately 150,000 families were eligible for wage subsidies, according to the city welfare department's estimates, but only about 15,000 families were claiming them.

The total of the ineligible but poor, plus the eligible non-recipients, plus the eligible but fully employed recipients is large. One can juxtapose it to the number of able-bodied, unemployed recipients — after subtracting from the latter figure all the dependent children and aged persons it includes — and arrive at figures most unhelpful to the argument that welfare programs cosset a mob of lazy apostates who mock the Protestant Ethic.

Meantime, the facts available on the attitudes toward work of typical welfare recipients — man, woman, or even dependent child — suggest that President Nixon's formulation of the "welfare ethic" as against the "work ethic" is seriously flawed. A 1972 study, by the staid Brookings Institution, of the "work orientations" of the poor demonstrates that the poor as a body share with more prosperous Americans all those beliefs in employment, incentives, and rewards which the President claimed, in his celebrated Labor Day speech, help "build strong people" while "the welfare ethic breeds weak people." Welfare recipients, according to the Brookings study, viewed public assistance with favor — with *mild* favor — only *after* they had experienced serious occupational failures; these failures the researchers found attributable to labor-market conditions, not to the inadequacies of those who had become public charges. There is simply no evidence in this competent investigation (which took account of possible disparities between what respondents said and what they actually did about work) that we shelter from the chill winds of the marketplace large numbers of poor people who subscribe to what the President knows is out there: ". . . the new 'welfare ethic' that could cause the American character to weaken."

Some observers might even argue that our welfare policies tell a far sadder story about the values of the architects of these policies, and about the constituencies who encourage them, than about attitudes toward work in the larger population. Others might add, with Calvin Coolidge, that "the reason we have such high unemployment rates is that there aren't enough jobs." And carrying a suspicion of current policy a bit further, what should we make of the "workfare" concept? Does this considerable effort to get poor mothers of young children off the "aid-to-dependent-children" rolls serve the Ethic? Or do our national income accounts, which assign no economic value at all to child-rearing, give testimony to an enduringly narrow and highly selective application of the Ethic's prescriptions?

Our several logics, and our tendency to infer favored conclusions from selective facts, may suit our continuing need to equate necessity with morality. Can that be why no one suggests that the tenets of the faith have been toyed with by its own most ardent — and its most powerful — followers? Corporations, in whose corridors march the most articulate proponents of the Ethic, face "the worst attitude climate in a decade," according to the Opinion Research Corporation, a subsidiary of the McGraw-Hill Company, whose own journal, *Business Week,* editorializes on the facts of a survey as follows:

[Reversal of public disaffection with business] will take management that thinks in terms of long-run objectives rather than
short-run profits. Much of the trouble that business has got into
during the past five years has developed because executives were
watching the security analyst and playing for a quick flash in
the stock market instead of building for the future. Now the
future they did not prepare for is here.

Deferred gratification? Saving for growth? The *Business
Week* data on public attitudes toward business might well
unsettle the *Business Week* editors. These data show that the
"staunchest supporters" of business have an increasingly low
opinion of extant businesses; the proportion of respondents
reporting "low approval of companies" is 60 percent, up nearly 15 percentage points since 1965. In the same issue, *Business
Week* provides a handy if incomplete summary of the reasons
for this. It is a grim litany of rapacious conglomerates, "hu-
miliating miscalculations" in aerospace, I.T.T. in the Justice
Department, junk in the environment, and plain shoddy
merchandise.

Try as they will to be objective about an important matter, however, *Business Week* cannot resist pronouncing a curse
on the other house — a comfort to those executive subscribers
who brood upon workers and the Protestant Ethic. Thus, two
tables purport to show that of late "people want more for
less." These same tables are captioned: "They will not work
harder to increase their standard of living, but they say they
could produce more if they tried." Sure enough, the proportion of worker-respondents who "say they could produce
more if they tried" can be seen to have risen appreciably
since the late nineteen-forties. From this, *Business Week* con-
cludes that more and more workers want a higher standard
of living but refuse to work harder for it. But a careful inspection of the tables and the several captions could as easily
support the interpretation that larger numbers of respondents
are content with their standard of living, thanks all the same,
and in that respect see no purpose in working harder.

Indeed, in not yearning after new feats of consumption
these workers seem well within the Ethic, which never did
put much stock in consuming but urged, instead, deferred

gratification. Poor Richard could not have envisioned Miami Beach, and Horatio Alger knew not Neiman-Marcus. Conversely, of course, any society whose citizens consistently deferred their pleasures in the interests of security, liquidity, and growth would find little place for, say, credit-granting institutions and advertising agencies.

All in all, it seems a waste of good elbow-grease for the executive classes to wring their hands unduly over the apostasy of workers from the Ethic. Perhaps the least consolable have read the April 1972 Gallup Poll, to which 57 percent of the "total public" admitted that ". . . they could produce more each day if they tried." But did those same executives notice that the figure for professional people and businessmen was *70 percent?* Only one group felt less productive still: the 72 percent of young people between 18 and 29 years old.

These last statistics suggest (though they do not prove; "for instance" is not proof) that the question of legitimacy higher up is an important one. Corporate shenanigans, political deceptions, and a professional-executive class avowedly and conspicuously underworked, may simply not inspire the larger population to seek "success" in the old way. One wonders if all of Madison Avenue's capacities for persuasion could blot out what millions see in their work-a-day lives: basic industries that turn tidy profits while great portions of their productive capacity stand idle through business-cycle swings; huge, unearned subsidies for inefficient aerospace firms; expense-account juggling, rapid corporate tax write-offs, and oil depletion allowances; railroads managed into bankruptcy; industrial wastes managed into rivers and lakes. It is naive to believe that the non-executive population is unaware of these things. Even *Playboy* has presented its leaders with a compendium of bare facts on the subject of malpractices. In a recent article Senator Philip A. Hart reviewed case after depressing case of mismanagement, managerial skullduggery, and breach of faith. Among the items: the nation's 70 largest corporations have run afoul of anti-trust, false advertising, patent, copyright, and labor laws 980 times in a 45-year period; of the 980, "779 indicated that crimes had been committed."

Nor does it please earners to be told, most often by their elected leaders, that it is their wages and salaries which are to blame for an inflationary spiral that has very nearly consumed the economic gains of many years. Wage-earners know that war is simultaneously expensive and unproductive, and many are also mindful of the spiraling costs of government. James W. Kuhn has pointed out that

> Philadelphia pays its clerical employees a third more than the average paid in private industry, and in both Houston and Buffalo clerks' pay is a fifth larger; municipal data processors earn salaries about a fifth larger than those employed by private firms in Philadelphia, Newark, and Los Angeles; and maintenance workers in New York and Newark average 42 percent larger salaries than those in private industry.

Government is expensive in other ways: wage-earners in New Jersey must read that their Secretary of State has been indicted for exploiting his office to line his pockets on the very eve of his predecessor's incarceration for the same behavior; this, only months after Newark's former mayor and some other public servants had been jailed for similar violations of the public trust.

Yet we are continually warned that the wage-earners subvert the work ethic. The journalist, recently published in *Reader's Digest,* who spent "much of 1971 . . . interviewing 500 representatives of construction companies" so as to inveigh against work-rules, unaccountably missed the wholesale corruption, involving builders and New York City inspectors, documented in *The New York Times* in the same month that *Reader's Digest* exposed the workers.

To put it judiciously, evidence that workers are misbehaving as never before is less than abundant. All the recently fashionable conferences on "work alienation" and "the changing work ethic," and all the front-page reports of H.E.W. studies of work and workers, would have us believe that there is a new crisis, and that productivity has suddenly given way to job turnover, industrial conflict, and worse. Yet the "quit rate" per 100 workers in manufacturing went *down* from 2.7 in 1969 to 1.8 in 1971, the last full year for which data are available. (Data on other employees are not recorded by the

Bureau of Labor Statistics; exceedingly few managers have trend data on white-collar workers, or consider them if they have them.) And President Nixon reminded us, in his Labor Day speech, that "today, we have achieved an era of relative calm on the labor-management front, with work stoppages at a six-year low."

Now it would be quite wrong to suppose that there are not some complex difficulties connected with work in contemporary American society. There are organizations in which absenteeism, turnover, conflict, and other offenses against productivity are of some moment, and the causes of these and other problems deserve systematic study. But it is well to view with skepticism all simplified explanations that focus only and owlishly on the worker's philosophy, and to examine a number of the currently popular prescriptive solutions with care.

Consider, for example, that E. Daniel Grady, division traffic manager for Michigan Bell Telephone Company, reduced the absenteeism of Detroit operators from 7½ percent to 4½ percent in one quarter by keeping attendance records on a weekly rather than a monthly basis. Mr. Grady, after digging into the matter, discovered that the telephone operators felt that a month's record had already been marred if they were absent early in that month; in for a penny, they went in for a pound. By recording in a shorter unit, he removed that easy rationale for multiple absences. And Edward J. Feeny, a vice-president of Emery Air Freight Corporation, was able to increase his employees' care and skill at packing cargo containers to capacity by the staggeringly simple expedient of *telling* the workers the difference in profits between filling to 45 percent and filling to the 90 percent they quickly achieved. The result: a $520,000 annual cost reduction. These illustrations could be multiplied to a degree that is dumbfounding; they may be found in any second-rate textbook on "human relations."

The plain truth is that the overriding majority of Americans are not lazy malcontents who soldier on the job at every opportunity. Even auto workers, universally famous for having the best reasons to be unhappy with their work, *act* upon their disenchantments with surprising inconsistency. Only about half of the production workers employed by the Big Three retire before reaching 65, according to Melvin Glasser, director of the U.A.W., Social Security Department. This, despite a "30 and out" retirement plan for workers 58 or older with 30 years service. Many keep working for financial reasons — to maintain pre-retirement pay and to benefit, ultimately, from any expansion in retirement benefits. The indication, says Mr. Glasser, is that the retirement age will be lowered, but he does not believe it will be lowered much.

We have dissatisfied workers in America, but work dissatisfaction is not laziness or historico-cultural sabotage. One might expect management, at so late a date, to know that. But that is another matter — for, as some of the observations in these paragraphs suggest, there are grounds for doubt about *managers'* willingness, in any sector of the economy, to get on with it. Dissatisfied workers may well become less productive in the face of evidence that managers don't know what they are doing themselves; evidence that employers are so protected from market pressures that they can afford to be inefficient; evidence that they will blame employees for their own miscalculations; or evidence that managers will seek to deceive the workers.

It is interesting to note in this regard that the single most frequent complaint listed by employees in a University of Michigan study was over the difficulty of getting their jobs done and done properly amid faulty materials, badly scheduled deliveries, and other manifestations of mismanagement. The second largest category of job dissatisfactions involved health and safety hazards, the overriding majority of which are wholly under management's control.

Readers unfamiliar with life in the basic industries might contemplate the experience of workers with avoidable occupational accidents and illnesses. In 1968, a total of 14,300 people died in industrial accidents — about the equivalent of American fatalities in Vietnam that year. "In the same year," report Patricia Cayo Sexton and Brendan Sexton,

90,000 workers suffered *permanent impairment* from industrial accidents, and a total of 2,100,000 suffered total but temporary disability.... In 1969 [exposures to industrial pollutants in the workplace] caused one million new cases of occupational disease. Among the casualties were 3,600 dead and over 800,000 cases of burns, lung and eye damage, dermatitis, and brain damage.

It is simply fatuous to believe that managers whose employees have an intimate, daily association with unnecessary risks to life and limb should be thought competent, never mind "legitimate," by those same employees. The "staunchest supporters" of industry questioned by *Business Week* may consult the front page of *The Wall Street Journal* for August 5, 1969, where an executive pronounced, "When you come right down to it, a lot of our safety decisions are really cost decisions. We give our workers safety glasses because they cost just $3.50. Safety shoes, which they also need, cost $14. . . ."

It is equally fatuous to believe that the current rash of experiments in "work enlargement" or "work enrichment" will fool workers anywhere when these programs are only ostensibly designed to enhance satisfaction in work. Well-intentioned social scientists who lecture managers on the currently favored techniques for elevating the "self-actualization" of workers may be in deeper than they know. Mr. Edwin Mills, director of the "Quality of Work Program" of the much touted National Commission on Productivity, told a Chicago business audience, just before the turn of the year, that 80 percent of 150 firms currently conducting experiments designed to "enlarge" and "enrich" work were non-union. Their managers reported in a private poll, according to Mr. Mills, that these experiments were part of such firms' over-all anti-union policy. It is doubtful, on historical grounds, that the dissatisfactions and needs which move workers to collective bargaining will be dissipated by "self-actualization." And deceptions will not help; employees will not be blinded to management incompetence by such strategies.

The fact is that management has lately become far more visible to the American employee, and the close-up is not flattering. The sociologist Fred Goldner has argued compellingly that the growing ranks of managers have themselves become a work-force of extraordinary magnitude. Managers' habits, their technical competence, and their dedication to work are on display as never before, and are as open to interpretation as their workers'. Particularly in a "service economy," in which so many of us "work with our heads," it is not difficult to justify visits to the barber shop or the hairdresser as being, so to speak, continuing work toward the same end. After all, "the mind doesn't punch in and out," and "we're really working all the time." To the extent that we believe and act on that premise we will be observed doing so. That is, we will ourselves be judged by the rest of our countrymen who have brought their ascetic heritage into a convenient — a necessary — synthesis with the impulse toward comfort.

It was Max Weber, the German sociologist and economic historian, who explored most fully the role of the Protestant Ethic in the genesis of capitalism. And it was Weber who examined at length, in his studies of authority, the concept of legitimacy. He concluded that in large, complex organizations, technical competence was a central inducement to the acceptance of authority by subordinates. Weber might see, in those facts of contemporary American life I have touched on, signs of damage, not to the ethic that stimulates workers under legitimate conditions, but to management's claim to the loyalty and industrious output of its millions of charges.

PART THREE

Coping:
Unions and Management

The New Workers – A Report

by John Haynes

Skipper, twenty-six years old, has been working since he was eighteen, the last four years as a fork lift operator at a large upstate New York plant. He is a union steward, the youngest in the plant. His fellow stewards still call him "the punk" even after two years in office. Skip has many complaints against the older generation, among them its refusal to "let me in on the action."

He does "as little as possible" and wants an easier life. "Money isn't everything any more. You can always make ends meet. I want to see us get thirty years and out — you know, retirement after thirty years with the company. Man, I want to be out there doing my thing when I'm fifty."

Skip is adamant about the older people in the plant. "They all live in the past. They laid a good groundwork in the past, so why don't they relax and reap the harvest? The old are always sounding off about how we have it so easy. So what. They helped make it that way for us. They are always bugging me about my hair. So, I let it grow longer. You know, when I started here at $2.00 an hour it really worried them. They really thought I should be getting 80¢ like they did." This young worker has a catalog of complaints. Yet, he is an active union steward and is anxious to run for higher office in the local. "Man, we'll change a few things around here then."

When I started work twenty-two years ago I was struck by the fact that everyone shared my dream of getting out of

Reprinted with permission from *New Generation*. Copyright © 1970 by the National Committee on Employment of Youth.

the shop. Everyone had a pet dream — opening a luncheon-ette, becoming a photographer or a salesman. We all shared that one ideal — get out of the plant. Of course, very few did. In a recent tour, every young worker I talked to spoke about getting out of the shop. "I've been here four months and that's four months too long. I'm going back to school." The dream has not changed over the twenty-two years. The change is in the method of getting out. More education is seen as the practical way out. The desire is as strong as ever and most young workers dream of the college route to a better life.

I stood watching eighteen-year-old Red drive home three screws with an air gun and wondered if that was why he had a high school diploma. "Do you feel that this is the kind of work you went to high school for?" I asked him. "Yep, all the work is pretty much the same wherever you go. You can't get into any of the plants around here unless you've finished high school."

This fact distinguishes the younger worker from the older generation in terms of attitude, vision and satisfaction. No diploma was necessary twenty years ago to drive home three screws. The new workforce is more highly educated, wants even more education, is more articulate, more tolerant of others, less fearful about its own future. The past fifteen years of relatively stable employment has meant that few of them have had any experience with joblessness in their entire lifetime. They don't share their elders' fear of unemployment. They are untouched by the 1930's, confident that "I'll make out." The older generation cannot escape from the impact of the thirties; no matter how long the current swing of high employment lasts, they are sure that "It'll come to an end soon — and then you'll see." This difference in experience also separates the two groups of workers and lays the groundwork for friction now and substantial changes of union policies in the future.

The friction between the generations makes it difficult to talk to younger workers. There is an inherent mistrust that is overcome most easily in a bar over a few beers. Interviews on the production line or in the union office elicit standard responses that they think you want to hear. In a more social atmosphere among their peers they talk freely and openly about their feelings.

Almost all of the grievances in the plant involving workers concern discipline. "If the young fellows don't get what they want, they raise hell with the steward, the foreman and everyone else." The older worker, partly due to his lifelong fear of unemployment, his lack of education and articulateness, tends to accept whatever the company hands out. The younger worker constantly fights it. One common complaint about modern factory work life stems from a very different concept of a fair day's work for a fair day's pay. In the past, the union has contented itself with establishing a fair day's pay, leaving the employer to set a fair day's work. The young worker wants to help set both standards.

A middle-aged steward told of a recent case in his section. Three young workers, age twenty and twenty-one, were hired on the second shift to clean the offices. One evening the foreman caught one of the young janitors doing his homework (he went to school during the day) ; another was reading the paper and the third was asleep with his feet up on the desk. The foreman exploded and gave them a written warning. The workers filed a grievance protesting the warnings. "We cleaned all the offices in five hours by really hustling and who the hell should get upset because then we did our own thing," one of them said. Art, who hopes to be an engineer, told me that "at school during study period I get my studies done in less than the hour and no one bugs me when I do other things for the rest of the time. We cleaned all those offices in five hours instead of eight. What more do they want?"

The steward said he tried hard to understand what they were saying. "But the company has the right to expect eight hours work for eight hours pay," he repeated. "I finally got the kids to understand by taking them outside and telling them that if they got the work finished in five hours, then the company would either give them more work or get rid of one of them. They're spacing it out nicely now and everyone's happy," he said, satisfied to have settled the grievance within the understood rules. The young workers are not so happy. They are living with the rules but they want them changed. They want eight hours work to be established and then they want the freedom to operate within those eight hours however they see fit, as professionals do.

Another grievance in the same plant illustrates this changing attitude towards productivity. The grievance of a worker protesting a warning notice tells the story. "At approximately 11 (11:17 till 11:30 clean up and punch out) Bill B., the foreman, approached Tom M., the bracket welder, on the tub line and asked him why he wasn't running his job. M. told the foreman he was pacing himself and according to his count (downtime and running time) he had already run more than a fair night's work which came to a total of 8.2 hours. The foreman told M. he had to stay on the job till 11:17 and went on to tell him about other company rules that had to be followed. M. told the foreman he didn't feel it was right for him to have to go back on the son-of-a-bitch, since he had already done his job according to his figures."

The worker's response to the foreman's demand is part of a deeper demand for recognition of individual worth. Few young workers are willing to be considered clock numbers or parts of the machine. Each recognizes himself as an individual and wants to be treated as one. They have a self-confidence born of security. "I'm a good worker; why get on my back if I quit early." They consider themselves equal to any man in the plant. If the foreman is abusive, they'll be abusive right back. "We don't take any nonsense from any foreman. He gets more pay than us and that's OK but we don't have to grovel to him like the old guys do."

In the case just described it is probable that Tom used stronger words than "son-of-a-bitch," because the worker also received a warning for using abusive language. The company response to Tom's grievance stated, "Insubordination and abusive language cannot and will not be tolerated. Whenever such a situation does occur, disciplinary action will follow." But the company does not take the same position when the complaint is the other way around. Young workers are quick to point out the double standard. Around the same time, the workers in the next department filed a grievance against their foreman protesting "this use of vulgar, profane and defaming language that Mr. N. used in referring to one of his employees, Paul N." The company response to that grievance was: "It is not the company's intent for management to use profane language to hourly employees." And, there the matter was closed. But, the young workers say they intend to pursue this and to file other grievances against foremen who "try to push us around." This does not mean that young workers object to "shop talk." They do object to it being used as a managerial tool.

Many foremen complain about the problem of maintaining discipline in the plant among the younger workers. "I have to watch these younger guys; they talk back to me. And if I push them too hard, they seem to gang up on me and start things rolling in the section to cause an uproar." The steward bore this out. "When you get before the company with these younger guys, they really fight. They talk up and argue for their rights. The older guys speak only when asked a question; the kids want to take charge of their own cases. You know, the older people prefer to forget the problem and wait for it to blow over. The younger guys fight it even if it's not going on their records. Hell, they do a good job for themselves."

The atmosphere in any plant is set by the way the union fights the company rules. If the union agrees to them as acceptable guidelines, they become the norm for everyone. The younger worker rebels against such a norm. Most young workers feel hemmed in by company rules and regulations set by the older generation in line with older values. They object to older people deciding how younger ones should operate. And the two generations' very different experiences may lead to sharp conflict.

For example, the company sets the admissible level of absenteeism. Older people accept whatever the company sets. The younger worker does not. Harry, twenty-one, has been working on the line for less than a year. "A couple of months ago the foreman had two men working on the line above me. They were doing more than I could handle, so I called the foreman over and told him to get me some help. He told me I could do the job if I hustled my ass. I took this for about an hour more and then just quit. I punched out at 6 (5½ hours early) on Wednesday and stayed home till the following Monday. I got me a doctor's certificate that I had sprained my ankle on Thursday morning but they still got me for quitting early on the Wednesday. They gave me a three-day suspension. But, I didn't mind because it was summer and it's hot working here. I did some fishing and sleeping and really enjoyed it."

Most of the single men I met tend to take extra time off. Since the seniority provisions apply to choice of shift, most younger workers are on the second and third shifts which usually pay a ten per cent shift differential. Their average wage is $125 to $175 a week, depending on the hourly rate. In the auto industry, where the average rate is over $4 an hour, the single worker on the second shift can make $100 in three days. The frequent opportunities for overtime at premium rates mean a full pocket and the urge to take off at the end of the week. The major auto manufacturers have resigned themselves to hiring numbers of students on the Monday and Friday shifts to make up for the high absenteeism on these two days.

Many of the young workers who said they were going back to school added, "as soon as I've finished paying for the car and put a little money aside." But, from their tone of voice you know they will never accumulate that little extra — even if they pay off the car before needing a new one. Despite his change in attitude towards production, the young worker is still very much a consumer in our consumer-oriented society.

The young married worker with a child has real problems. His earnings are less than fifty cents an hour higher than the newly hired single man. Because he has family responsibilities, he can't take the day off; he can't afford to reject the overtime; he can't afford a three-day suspension for breaking the rules. He shares the sense of freedom that pervades his generation but he can no longer exercise it.

There is a myth of worker affluence in America. Most

people think that workers have made it. Yet, $3.50 an hour — a respectable wage in most plants — is only $7,280 a year, almost $4,000 less than the Bureau of Labor Statistics' estimate of an adequate but average standard of living for an urban family of four. Almost all the married workers I talked to had working wives and many also held down second jobs. Many families with children have worked out some child care arrangement so that the wives could also work to help maintain a decent income. In effect, working America is not affluent but hard working. Almost all of the younger workers saw a need for day care centers close to the plant. Most thought the union could do something about this.

The young married worker sees the possibilities for change through the union. He is beginning to sense production line work as a permanent way of life. "My wife and I have talked about my going back to school on and off for the last three years, but things keep coming up," said twenty-six-year-old Leo. "You should look around for the education before you come to work, because once you're here it's tough to get out." He is a typical young worker, married with one child and another on the way. He went through the 110-day strike at General Electric and, along with his colleagues, stayed with the union. His steward, John Shumate, also twenty-six, was in charge of the pickets during the strike. He reported that all of his members — and all of his generation — stood with the union throughout the 110 days. "Young guys see the advantage of the union. I have few problems signing them up and they stick with the union all along the way," he told me.

Older stewards supported this. "You have more problems signing up the older guys who want an explanation and then want to be convinced; the younger guys take the union card and sign it up without any arguments. They're not afraid of the company." The union at General Electric operates under an open shop — union membership is voluntary. Yet, at the Louisville plant where half of the workforce is under thirty-five, 97 per cent of the workers are in the union. In another plant with the union shop a middle-aged steward said, "The kids understand the union. There's no problem about dues; they never complain about the dues. But, the young guy wants his rights and he's going to get all of them."

Leo shares the general view that the grievance machinery is effective but too slow and cumbersome. "It is also one-sided. If the company disciplines a worker, the penalty is put into effect immediately and the individual grieves it." For example, a worker given a three-day suspension for "bad work" gets the three days off without pay. He protests this through the grievance procedure. If the case goes to arbitration, it can take over a year for a final ruling. Even those decisions reached before arbitration usually take over six months to resolve. If the ruling is in favor of the worker, he receives his three days' pay. But, young workers don't like to wait. "Why can't they file a grievance against us and, if we are proven guilty, then they can dock us. It doesn't seem right to have them find us guilty and then hold the hearings." On the other side of the coin, young workers express irritation that the company can unilaterally do things that are stopped only after the union wins a grievance. "The company has it coming and going," protest many young workers.

Leo thinks that seniority is important to his future. "You might need a little flexibility in the more skilled jobs because the older guys are set in their ways. But, seniority is important to me because I know that no one can come in off the street and take my job away from me. I've worked my way up to one of the easier jobs on the line and I want to keep it." All of the young workers I talked to supported the basic idea of seniority (except some skilled workers who were just completing their apprenticeships). They look for increased opportunities through a higher turnover. The UAW demand of "thirty years and out" is popular among the younger workers. They are motivated partly through the desire to limit the number of years they have to put in on the production line and partly from the knowledge that, if the older workers retire after thirty years regardless of age, then they will get a crack at the better jobs held by the higher seniority members.

The military experience has helped focus attention on

early retirement. Ronnie, twenty-four, and just returned from a four-year hitch with the Navy, spoke about early retirement. "In the military you get out after twenty years. If it's good enough for them, I guess it's good enough for civilian life."

The main complaint of young workers against seniority concerns determining fringe benefits. "Why should I have to wait for ten years and I'm too old to enjoy the third week's vacation. When it comes to vacations, seniority is a lot of crap," a twenty-two-year-old drill press operator said vehemently. They understand the value of seniority in computing job rights but they want to share in the fringe benefits of older workers right now. Most thought this is one area where the unions could push harder. "It's our money they use to buy those extra vacations for the older guys. It's time we got some of it," said one low-service employee.

A great deal has been written about industrial sabotage and carelessness of younger workers, angered over their working conditions. In general, I did not find this. Rather, they frequently complained about production techniques that turned out shoddy products. One group told me of being ordered to substitute parts and even, in one case, to omit a part that was short rather than close down the line. "That's not fair, because the guy that buys that is not getting his money's worth." I found a great deal of product pride and an attempt to identify with the work, even though the individual contribution was insignificant. The sense of a good job well done still holds with younger workers, even where they are tightening down three screws for eight hours a day. Often, whether this feeling exists is directly related to the production pressures on the line. In an auto plant, where production is god and the workers are constantly pushed and harassed by the foreman to maintain the quota, the attitude towards the product is hatred. In other plants, where the pace is not so harsh, workers tend to feel more warmly about their products.

Many of the younger married workers complain about their paychecks. They are the most squeezed by the inflation and the lure of advertising to accumulate more than they can pay for. But, in Louisville where a massive General Electric plant competes for labor with a large Ford assembly plant, workers often have other criteria for taking a job. The Ford plant pays up to a dollar an hour more than the GE plant, but work in the auto assembly line is hard and rugged. Schedules are posted and maintained. Visits to the rest room are closely supervised. I asked a number of GE workers who complained about their paychecks why they chose to work at that plant rather than the auto factory. They all responded that their plant was more human. "Sure you get paid more over there, but man, you work your ass off for it."

Few young workers seem to select their jobs with any particular thought. "I was looking for a job and I found this one." With full employment and little sense of direction, most high school graduates drift into the plant that already employs friends and relatives. Only after he has the job does he decide whether he wants to keep it. Turnover is extremely high in the under twenty-five age group. Many of them aim to stay at a plant for one year, "make a little bread and split." A month off work and then drift back into another plant.

Increasingly, career jobs are being blocked to high school graduates. John Shumate, the young steward who would also like to go back to school, wondered what was going to happen to the fellows who were following him in high school. "You read about the police department wanting college graduates for the police force. You see the clerical jobs becoming more and more technical with computers and the civil service entrance requirements going up and you wonder where it will all end. Will we all have to have a college education just to work?" He maintains many of the hard work values of his parents' generation. He wants to do a good job at whatever he is doing. That is probably why he is a union steward. It is a position that gives him an opportunity to work in a more meaningful way than his job on the line. He is not sure about student demonstrators but he shares his generation's greater tolerance of them.

Tolerance of the other person's individuality is a hallmark of this generation. Many of them are influenced by the now culture. Many wear their hair down to the shoulders. Most of the younger workers maintain a benign aloofness from the older generation. They prefer to "do their own thing," not worrying anyone and not being worried by anyone. Among the older workers, alcoholism is a problem. "You never see a young guy drunk," said a steward, "they seem to have a self-discipline to know when to stop." However, marijuana use appears to be growing among the younger generation. One foreman told me that he saw a group of workers passing a joint around during a coffee break. "When I was their age we would sneak a cigarette and worry about it. Nowadays, they are much more open and daring."

Hard drugs are also creeping in. It is very difficult to get any accurate data because few people want to talk about the problem. The president of a local at an elevator plant told me of a "clean cut kid who took a job as messenger. Paid about $80 a week. He was really a nice looking kid — short hair, neat, you know, just like our kids. Well, at the end of the first week he began flashing a big roll of money around. I knew he wasn't earning it on his job. So, we kept a watch on him. The security people caught him selling heroin. He took that job just to be able to move about the plant and reach his contacts." The same union official thought that there were at least twenty hard addicts working at the plant which employs a couple of thousand people.

Frequently, the union, run by the older generation, is caught by its own attitudes into supporting outmoded company rules. Many disputes over hair length still occur. Company officials don't see it as a company versus worker problem but rather a generational one. Don Rock, president of the local union in Louisville, is very sensitive about the rights of his younger members. Recently a foreman told a young member to get his hair cut because, "the union president agrees with us that you should." Rock said that as soon as he found out about it he let the foreman and the member know that "I don't give a damn how he cuts his hair, that's his right." This defense of the younger members' rights is reflected in the attitudes of the young members. There were fewer complaints about work, the union and life in general at the

Louisville plant on the part of the younger members. His experience is borne out by Victor Gotbaum, President of District Council 37 of the State, County and Municipal Workers Union in New York City. "The young clerical workers flooding into our union are becoming our backbone. They have a real sense of unionism, these young people," Gotbaum said.

Work on the production line has not changed much over the years. It is still dirty, heavy and monotonous. Even the new plants are only airy and clean in the office areas. The production line is still marked by loud noise, grease and oil on the floors, trash cans in the aisles, intense heat from the machinery and deadly monotony due to the breakdown of the job into its simplest components and the constant push of the ever-moving production line.

Automation, or the less exotic mechanization, has not reduced the hard slog of work for many people. Paychecks are still too small for the family man. The work is even more dehumanizing. The role of the union in humanizing work is as important as ever. The basic problems facing workers have not changed over the last thirty years, nor have their attitudes basically changed. But the opportunities for expressing them have.

The younger worker can stand up and be counted as an individual. He does not have to say Yes to everything the foreman tells him. He does not live with the fear of the depression. He does not see the need for working five days a week nor the virtue in working fifty weeks a year. He does not see himself as a slave to his machine. Rather, he feels he has contracted to produce eight hours work and it's up to him how he does it. He is as close to his union and as far from his boss as his father was in 1935. He is willing to strike to win his rights which are more personalized than the collective demands of the 1930's.

He finds that the older generation does not share many of his aspirations. However, he is moving into union positions. At present he is the isolated steward. Occasionally he is an area representative. In ten years he will be the shop chairman of the local union and probably its president. He will shape the attitudes of the local. He will determine which company prerogatives the union will challenge. He is going to be more insistent on individual rights. He will seek greater control over the work rules, immediate application of fringe benefits, and the right to work a lot less than eight hours a day, five days a week, fifty weeks a year.

Labor: The Anti-Youth Establishment

by Lewis Carliner

Arthur Hinkle, 28-year-old white factory worker, and Bradford Jones, 23-year-old black factory worker, are two rank-and-file soldiers in a guerrilla war now being waged in the labor movement. At the moment the war is still sputtering; it hasn't fully broken out. Except for occasional flareups not always recognized as incidents in the war — the Wallace vote in some areas, the rejection of newly negotiated union agreements by the rank and file, the revolutionary unity movement among auto workers in Detroit — the shape of the conflict is only beginning to become visible.

Hinkle and Jones, it needs to be said immediately, are both fighting the old men — in the plant, in the union, in the community and in the society. But because the best indications are that they don't yet know that this is what they are battling, they are not fighting side by side. Indeed, sometimes they are fighting each other.

Young American workers like Hinkle and Jones are older than other people we define as young in the United States and much older than young workers overseas, where 16-year-olds and sometimes 15-year-olds go into factories to work as apprentices. In the United States young factory workers are generally defined as between 23 and 35. This makes the youngest factory worker older than the oldest student, except for graduate students.

This age difference accounts for part of the lack of understanding between young workers and students, although both have their backs up against the going establishment.

Reprinted with permission from *New Generation*. Copyright © 1969 by the National Committee on Employment of Youth.

Class differences, resulting in widely opposite cultural and political attitudes, are another major factor. But even though they don't realize it, young workers, students and black youth all have the same basic grievances. What escapes them, and affects them all, unequally but powerfully, is that the economic differences between young and old are generally more marked than differences between worker and boss, or black and white. The disparity in the situation between young and old is heavily weighted to the advantage of people over 35. Bureaucratic dynamisms have operated to give the older men control over the agencies in the society which in ordinary circumstances conduct protest activities: unions, political parties, institutionalized reformist agencies. The slogan "Never trust anyone over 30," which when it was first raised seemed to be a joke, is actually based on an empirical understanding of the treatment accorded by those over 30 to those under.

The under-35 grievances are simple and inescapable, once they are looked at squarely. Young workers, like students, have less money and power than older people although they often share the same responsibilities. The cries of students for participatory democracy and of blacks for self-determination have been heard across the country, but until recently there had only been mumbles of discontent from young workers. As would be expected, students and black people are far more articulate about what bugs them than are young workers.

But there are other reasons for lack of understanding about the problems of young workers.

Union newspapers, which represent the views of the union administration, deliberately do not air the grievances of young workers, nor do management publications. Young workers themselves have no organizations, as other dissident groups do, and no means for expressing their views except the traditional methods that workers have always invoked — repudiating their leaders and resorting to wildcat strikes.

There is currently a general belief that there has been a substantial increase in exuberantly violent wildcat strikes led and insisted upon by young workers. The strike at American Motors during 1967 is often cited as an example of the kind of strike that is almost, but not quite, an epidemic.

But there is better evidence of disaffection in the rejection of contract terms by the rank and file after they have been negotiated by union officers and staff. Nationally, the number of strike-settlement rejections has been rising steadily since 1964, the earliest year for which data is available.

"A common cause of these rejections," according to the director of the Federal Mediation and Conciliation Service, "is the advent of a young work force. Many young workers who have grown up in a period of relative affluence have never experienced either a real depression or the early history of union struggles. Moreover, they are not very interested in attempts to acquaint them with these hard facts of earlier years. Many have never experienced a strike of any duration. When these facts are coupled with what may be loosely described as the current disillusionment of youth in other areas of activity, negative ratification votes are not surprising."

The implication in this assessment is that young workers are talking back to their elders and betters because they have not experienced the hardships that older union members suffered in earlier struggles. It reflects an attitude that is the object of resentment of young students, workers and blacks throughout the country. The fact is that young people are a minority with the usual minority grievances: they are discriminated against in the matter of rewards and privileges, denied representation in the government of their society and its commercial and educational institutions, and required to be unwilling audiences to traditional declarations by the people in power that the protesters are too young, too inexperienced, too ignorant, too unprepared and in general too damned insolent to merit serious consideration.

Against the claim that young workers strike and reject contracts because they have never met a payroll or walked a picket line in the winter of 1938, there is clear evidence in the current work situation and economic data that young workers have serious causes for complaint.

Within the union structure itself, neither the locals nor the national and international unions even begin to give young people the representation on governing boards that they are entitled to on the basis of their numbers.

The seniority system and the instinct of people to hang onto their jobs in a bureaucracy account for the fact that the labor movement has become what might be called a gerontocracy. The movement which rejects the view that seniority qualifies superannuated Dixiecrats for chairmanships in the key congressional committees has not turned its attention to its own trade-union arteriosclerosis.

On the job, young workers, especially in their earliest days in the plant, understandably resent the seniority system and frequently claim that the local union leadership and plant management are in league against them in matters of the distribution of overtime, promotions and desirable transfers, and are deaf to such grievances connected with low seniority as having to work the second and third shift. Granted that the history of the trade-union movement is a powerful argument for the strongest possible seniority protection, other security provisions and full employment might still make it possible to give young people clearly defined opportunities to bypass seniority restraints in order to utilize a particular talent.

One characteristic of today's young workers that mocks the older workers' claim to know more and be wiser is the disparity in education between younger and older employees. At present, the majority of new employees are high school graduates and many have college training; in general they have better formal educations than those who deny them representation in the union.

Data compiled by both the unions and the Bureau of Labor Statistics reveal the importance of demographic facts to unions and the condition of workers, young and old. Each year some three million people enter the labor force and of these a third of the men and about a fifth of the women are employed in factories. In 1960 there were slightly more than 13 million people in the labor force under 25 and by 1970 this figure will have increased to almost 20 million. Workers over 45 will increase about 18.5 per cent in the same period, while workers in the 35-to-44 age group will decline. Thus labor leaders will soon have to deal with a constituency that is relatively old and relatively young, with the young in the majority.

The testimony everywhere in the society — especially in the political sphere, where grievances are the raw materials — is that young workers are being subjected to an intense propaganda attack against pensions and social security. In the plant they are told, very often by foremen, but by co-workers as well, that they are being taxed out of wage increases to provide pensions for the older workers.

Outside the plant management-sponsored organizations and right-wing political groups bombard them with literature that insists that the social security program is a fraud perpetuated against young workers, that if an amount equivalent to what they pay into social security were deposited in a savings bank it would pay them far more than they will ever receive in social security benefits, that the social security fund is bankrupt, and that they are being taxed to pay pensions to the aged today because of this bankruptcy. All these allegations are demonstrably untrue, but nevertheless increases in social security taxes have enraged young workers, especially since their own economic situation is not understood by the labor movement, the government, or even by the young worker himself.

Apart from the poor, no group in the society is under greater economic pressure than young workers. When they are told by their older co-workers in the plant that things have never been so good, wages higher, conditions better, vacations more satisfactory, and that all this is the result of the older workers' sacrifices, their reply is often, "So what? Things aren't all that good now." The truth is that for the younger worker things are *not* very good.

He spends on the average more than he earns and goes into debt each year. At the beginning of the Sixties he was going into debt on an average of $100 a year, and he is probably going more deeply into debt now. He sees taxes for pensions and social security as money he could use to pay his bills and keep even.

Wealth and financial well-being among American workers are closely related to the age of the worker and of his wife and children. In part this is because workers under 35 are usually married to women whose full-time occupation is raising children. During this period they are under the heaviest economic burden most Americans ever have to bear — buying a home, often paying off the borrowed down payment on the house, buying a car, furniture, appliances, paying for their children.

When their children reach the teens the situation changes. Often their wives return to work and the family income almost doubles; the house is substantially paid for; the installment accounts are paid off; bills are under control. Suddenly instead of pressure there is relative affluence.

The changing situation of the young worker growing old is revealed in Federal Reserve System statistics.

Families headed by persons under 35 had total assets valued at $6,304 in 1963, representing equity in a car, house, investments, insurance, and so forth. Scaled down by age, it is obvious that the assets of a family with a 25-year-old head who has one baby and another on the way come to very nearly nothing. Families with heads in the 35-to-44 age group are better off, with total average assets of $16,008, of which some $3,541 is invested, and with liquid assets of almost $5,000. Things are even better, financially, for the 55-to-64-year-old group, whose resources averaged $32,527 in 1963 and who had, among other assets, some $12,212 in investments and $6,401 in liquid assets.

The young worker has a two-edged grievance: he is under an impossible financial burden, and part of his burden is due to the fact that he must help provide for the far more well-to-do older worker. Moreover, in recent years this situation has been compounded by inflation, which on the whole has benefited American workers. But in the case of the younger worker it means that he must pay $3,000 to $5,000 more for a house than he would have had to pay two years ago. In addition, his mortgage exacts a usurious 7½ or 8 per cent interest in comparison with the 4 to 6 per cent the older workers are paying off. No wonder it seems to him that the entire society is a seniority swindle designed to victimize him.

Young workers in Sweden, Great Britain, Japan and a number of other countries are not tied in a bind that compels them to resent the pensions paid older workers. They receive housing assistance, grants on marriage, family allowances and a variety of services to help them surmount the mountainous costs of raising a young family.

Unions and political parties responsive to the needs of young constituents should have long ago devised a program to meet these problems. Yet even the student loans offered today become a further burden to the young father who has to repay them. Perhaps there should be very long-term loans for young families, with minimal payments in the first 15 years and high payments in the last 25 years when inflation and the improved economic position of being an older worker would operate to reduce the required payments to a nominal charge.

Possibly social security could be tied to family-assistance programs for young people, down payments on a house, interest subventions, grants to buy furniture and appliances and allowances for each child, so that the social security tax and pension deduction would be combined with benefits to the young as well as the old. Better still, loans to young workers could be paid back through a 1 per cent surtax on income beginning at age 35.

The unions should explore collective-bargaining ventures aimed at relieving the pressures on young people. But most important, the society and the labor movement should move to admit the young into the government of the community. Otherwise the anti-youth establishment may be confronted from another direction in the society by the cry of "Up against the wall, you old gerontocrats. . . ."

The Rebellious Rank and File

by John S. Greenebaum

On October 1, 1971, 100,000 soft-coal miners, their contract expired, put down their tools and walked off the job. But it wasn't the usual end-of-contract strike. United Mine Workers' president W. A. (Tony) Boyle didn't call it. The rank and file did — against the wishes of UMW leaders. This case of union membership and leadership at loggerheads is by no means an isolated one these days. Serious membership-leadership battles have taken place within the West Coast longshoremen's union, the giant 1.5-million-member United Steelworkers, and other unions.

Recently, there has also been a rash of antileadership confrontations in locals across the country. The extent of the schism was reflected in the New York City experience, after protracted and nerve-racking negotiations, when the leaders of the firemen, patrolmen, and sanitation workers privately admitted to the city council that their nerves were so racked by the prospect of having to head off militant elements in their memberships that they would be glad to agree to binding arbitration. (The result was the first binding-arbitration law in any major city.)

Labor leaders aren't the only ones for whom this dissident trend spells trouble; the increasing militancy of union membership poses major problems for management, too. In general, management views the labor movement as a nagging headache. Still, labor-management relations have enjoyed a measure of order and stability because, on the whole, union members did as the leadership told them to do. In the past,

Reprinted by permission of the publisher from *Personnel,* March-April 1972; © 1972 by the American Management Association, Inc.

contracts negotiated by labor leaders usually have received rubber-stamp approval from the membership.

Now, however, with growing frequency contracts union leaders recommend for approval are angrily rejected by membership and contracts are becoming less meaningful, less dependable, as self-assertive rank and file engage in illegal work stoppages and slowdowns. One result is that in negotiations of a contract affecting a militant rank and file, a common management tactic is the "nonfinal" final offer. Anticipating contract rejection, management makes what it terms its final offer, but actually holds back one or more concessions.

There is much more wrong than right with this tactic. First, it creates a credibility gap for management, as workers learn that management's final offer isn't final at all. They therefore think they have nothing to lose by routinely rejecting agreed-upon contracts until they become convinced they have driven management right to the wall.

Second, not knowing whether management is really making a final offer, union leaders are more and more inclined simply to send the contract to the membership, without recommending a course of action. This is, in effect, an abandonment of the union's role as negotiator. It puts control of the bargaining process in the hands of the workers, but more often than not, the workers are ignorant of the issues and of the long-term ramifications of their decisions.

When a disgruntled, unpredictable rank and file is in the picture, the best negotiating tactic for management is to make only one, *real* final offer and to back union leaders when, after agreement, they present it to their constituents. If the offer is rejected by the rank and file, management should not place any more offers on the table. There is the danger of a strike, of course, but the chances are that it will be a short one if it lacks the backing of union leadership.

Once a deal is hammered out between the company and the union bargainers, the company is doing no one a service by sweetening things up later on. Even if the immediate cost may be a work stoppage, to do otherwise would set a pattern of what might be called "rejection blackmail," to be repeated by the membership after negotiation.

Though taking a firm stand during bargaining is a sound tactic for management, it is defensive and stopgap; it does nothing to reduce the causes of rank-and-file discontent. Then how can management deal with it more positively? The answer requires an understanding of what is causing union membership and leadership to lock horns.

The gaping age difference between the leadership and the rank and file is one of the major reasons. For example, in the AFL-CIO, the majority of the leaders are in their 60s and 70s, whereas a large segment of the membership is in its mid-20s. Many of today's union leaders were the movement's driving organizers in the 1930s and 1940s, but members now complain that their leaders' drive is gone, that age and the good life have made them too soft, too conservative.

There is also a difference in attitudes toward work. Most union leaders vividly remember the hunger and widespread unemployment of the Depression that made a job precious, and to some extent, this experience still shapes their attitudes. On the other hand, younger union members, who entered the job market in times of relative affluence, don't share their leaders' reverence for employment. To them, a job is something they can always get, or even if they can't, one form or another of welfare will take care of them.

The younger members' confidence in security and mobility means that young workers want things now; they are not willing to wait five or ten years for a new car or twenty to thirty years for a house, as their parents did. Immediate benefits in dollars-per-hour carry far more weight with them than distant considerations like pensions and profit sharing.

The increasing number of blacks in the labor movement has also fueled the fires of rank-and-file unrest. It is estimated that from 10 to 15 percent of total labor union membership is black, and blacks are exerting the same pressures for equal or preferential treatment within the unions as they are in other societal structures. In some labor organizations — such as the United Automobile Workers, the United Steel Workers, the American Federation of Truckers — black caucuses have organized to give voice to what they believe are the special needs of the blacks. And other minorities — Puerto

Ricans and Mexicans, for example — are also forming pressure groups within various unions.

Still another factor is that union members are angry about their stagnant purchasing power, which, despite spectacular wage increases recently, hasn't increased perceptibly since 1965 because of inflation. Currently, the recession has made it impossible for union leadership to do anything about improving rank-and-file purchasing power.

To make jobs more stimulating and meaningful, many companies have tried job enrichment programs. While some of these have been short-term successes, most have been long-term failures, because most job enrichment programs simply replace a worker's single routine job with several equally routine ones. The variety stimulates the employee for a time, but a worker bored by one dull job soon becomes bored by several.

An exception to be noted is Motorola, which seems to be having some success with a job enrichment program in its Plantation, Fla. facility. There, each of the paging receivers of some 80 components is put together and packaged for shipment by a single assembly technician. Accompanying the receiver is a signed note from the assembler.

At present, productivity is up, turnover and absenteeism are down — but this has happened many times before. After an initial success, the novelty is likely to wear off and things slide back to where they were before.

In his book *The American Challenge*, Jean-Jacques Servan-Schreiber wrote:

> What, in the end, is management's most fundamental task? It is to deal with change. Management is the gate through which social, political, economic, and technological change—indeed, change in every dimension—is rationally and effectively spread through society. . . . Behind the success story of American industry lies the talent for accepting and mastering change.

If that is true, it is time management changed its attitudes toward and treatment of workers; there is no dealing with rank-and-file militancy otherwise.

Traditionally, the basic management approach has been to try to get workers to "think like management," to concern themselves with management's problems, such as cost control, productivity, and so on. By and large, workers haven't responded, and one of the main reasons is that most workers are almost totally absorbed by their own problems — the problems of getting by in an increasingly complex and fast-paced world.

Few workers — blue- or white-collar — are adequately equipped by education or experience to cope successfully with the complexities of life today: to get proper medical and dental care; to negotiate with landlords; to use credit wisely; to avoid an unjust debt; to get a friend out of jail; to provide for their children's education. Therefore, helping employees with their problems (which have hitherto been viewed as beyond a company's concern) is perhaps one of the most useful steps management can take to improve worker performance and reduce militancy.

For workers who need legal advice, a company could retain a lawyer to hold employee consultations on a regular basis. A company might also provide a counselor or a counseling team (perhaps of knowledgeable fellow employees) to give advice on family problems, on work difficulties, on where to obtain day care for children. In making such services available, the company would act as a clearing house, ensuring that the proper adviser or consultant teamed up with the employee seeking aid. Companies could also sponsor routine physical examinations, combined with information on how the employee and his family might obtain good medical and dental care. Still another area of company-sponsored advice might have to do with leisure time: golf, art, dancing, and music lessons for the employee or his children; how to get tickets to the theater, football games, other local sports events, and so on.

Furthermore, companies (particularly those with a large employee population) are increasingly tackling the graver problems of alcoholism and drug abuse. Management should not use the possibility of legal liability as an excuse to shy away from involvement in these employee problems. Even if the likelihood of liability is great, a company can still offer employees a referral service, instead of direct help. In locating the proper agency or professionals to help employees with their problems, a company could at the very least assist with correspondence and with the filling out of forms, both of which are difficult for many workers. If the experience of many newspapers and radio and TV stations offering what often amounts to a referral service is any indication, a corporate referral office could also provide valuable assistance to employees.

A company would also do well to consider new concepts that might benefit employees, such as the three- or four-day week, where the leisure time of the employee would be increased, presumably refreshing the employee after working on jobs that, of necessity, are dull and routine. Another possibility is a vacation with double pay, instead of straight time.

Obviously, all these ideas involve an element of cost. How can it be justified? Many, if not most, manufacturers are currently experiencing reductions in productivity, despite increased automation and official exhortations. This loss of productivity can clearly be traced to the attitude of the worker, the worker's lack of identification with the values of the employer — and here we come full circle: Labor can scarcely be expected to "think like management" until management, at least to some degree, thinks like labor.

Job Satisfaction I:
An Elusive Goal

by Thomas R. Brooks

American workers have been variously described as apathetic, authoritarian, contented, happy, inner-directed, other-directed — and now alienated. There is, most observers agree, considerable unease among Americans over the state of the economy, taxes, and a host of other problems.

Yet, if one takes job satisfaction as an index of alienation, or estrangement, Americans are remarkably content with their lot. A 1971 Gallup Poll showed 81 percent of all Americans expressing satisfaction with their jobs. However, for the first time since the question was first asked in 1949, there was a major drop in the job satisfaction poll, a fall of 6 percent from the 1969 high. The percentage of satisfaction had been increasing steadily, so a fall indicates that something has gone wrong.

When one considers, in addition, the other indices of disaffection — a rise in manhours lost in strikes, contract rejections, the vote for Alabama Gov. George Wallace, absenteeism and the like — there are grounds for concern. New urgency is given to some pertinent questions: Who is dissatisfied? Why? And what, if anything, ought to be done?

Trade unionists have a particular interest in the answers to these questions because, among other things, disaffection affects worker militancy as well as worker participation in their unions and in politics. All the surveys of dissatisfaction show that working people are more likely to be affected by "the blues" than the self-employed and those in technical, professional and managerial jobs, even though those occupations

Reprinted with permission from the *AFL-CIO American Federationist,* October 1972.

are not altogether exempt from the malaise. Only one in about 20 among the self-employed — and among construction workers — is dissatisfied as compared with about one in 10 among technical, professional and managerial people. But nearly one in four workers in the service and wholesale-retail industries expresses discontent with his job, and workers in manufacturing are not much happier.

Moreover, the various studies show that dissatisfied workers are likely to be more apathetic about their unions, least likely to play an active role and most likely to believe that their unions "do nothing." Discontented workers, too, loom large among those who, against the advice of their fellow workers, vote for George Wallace.

One must keep in mind, however, that the discontented are a minority among workers and within categories of workers — by age, income, industry, occupation, race and sex. Whether their number is growing or not, no one really knows. There are no studies over time. History, however, suggests that discontent rises and falls with ups and downs in the economy as well as with fluctuations in social temper and changes in the political climate. Broadly speaking, bad times generate bad feelings. Workers were never as affluent as John Kenneth Galbraith once thought they were. The median family income in 1968 was $8,632, about $1,000 short of what the Bureau of Labor Statistics called a "modest but adequate" income. Thanks to the trade union movement and substantial growth in total national income, however, the 1968 median was about $4,000 higher than that of 1947.

But the rising expectations generated by that increase were suddenly undercut by the erosion in real income among working people that began in the late 1960s. Buying power declined from 1965 to 1969 as pay envelopes were thinned by inflation and taxation. This erosion, coupled with recent economic uncertainties, rising unemployment and rising prices, lies behind the current rise in dissatisfaction evidenced in current academic studies of worker alienation.

The concept of alienation is of ancient lineage. It has been known throughout history and attracted the attention of thinkers of many eras. But whether dissatisfaction, disaffec-

tion or a vaguely defined and sensed malaise add up to alienation is a matter of dispute. Sociologists are sometimes rather
like Humpty Dumpty — "When I use a word, it means just
what I choose it to mean — neither more nor less." With this
and the qualifications about their number in mind, who are
the dissatisfied?

Late in 1969, the Survey Research Center at the University of Michigan, under contract from the Department of
Labor's Employment Standards Administration, conducted a
national survey of more than 1,500 currently employed workers. An able summary of the study's findings has been provided by Neal Q. Herrick, director of the Office of Program
Development at the Department of Labor, who provides more
details and analyses in *Where Have All the Robots Gone*,
which he edited with Dr. Harold L. Sheppard of the Upjohn
Institute. Most striking are the findings that appear to con-
firm the generation gap: By far and away, the most dissatisfied with their jobs were black workers under 30, with 37
percent expressing negative attitudes toward their jobs. The
second most dissatisfied group was workers age 29 and under
with some college education. Women under 29 were third.
Of the six most dissatisfied groups, all but one were made up
of workers age 29 and under. The exception was individuals
with some college education who earned less than $5,000 a
year.

Given the mass media's emphasis on the so-called youth
culture, the in-ness of youthful rebellion and the cachet of
long hair, pot and all the rest, what is truly surprising about
youth dissatisfaction is that it is so low. With the not unexpected exception of young blacks, no youth group mustered
more than 30 percent of their number as dissatisfied. Overall,
only 25 percent of young workers expressed negative feelings
toward their jobs. Admittedly, it is a sizable minority but one
whose outlook on life is brighter than the view of their immediate jobs. While there is a strong correlation between
those with negative attitudes toward work and those with
negative attitudes toward life, among the young the correlation was significantly weaker. Among those of ages 21 to 29,

barely 15 percent held negative attitudes toward life. Oddly, the very young — the 16 to 20 year olds — were more pessimistic: about 20 percent were negative toward life.

Work dissatisfaction appears to diminish as workers grow older, but whether this reflects a simple acceptance of a hard lot or the improvements that may come with growing older and gaining work experience remains in doubt as I read the survey findings. I suspect a little of both and perhaps more of the improvements through work experience. This can be deduced from the survey in part because income figures, which roughly reflect work skills, indicate that low-paid workers of all ages are more likely to be dissatisfied with their jobs than higher-paid workers. Only 13 percent of workers age 30 to 44 expressed negative feelings toward their jobs and the percentage drops as workers get older — 11 percent for those 45 to 54 and 6 percent for workers 55 and over. About one of every five workers making less than $5,000 a year was dissatisfied with his work, with the percentage dropping almost in half in the $5,000 to $10,000 range and down to 8 percent for those earning over $10,000 a year. As Herrick likes to say, "The old saying, 'I've been rich and I've been poor and believe me rich is better' remains valid today."

The color of your collar affects your chance of happiness on the job, according to the survey findings, with 17 percent of blue-collar workers expressing a negative attitude toward work as compared to 13 percent of their white-collar fellows. Significantly, an identical portion, 24 percent, of blue- and white-collar workers under 30 expressed dissatisfaction with their jobs. In the 30 to 44 age group, however, the percentage of dissatisfied white-collar workers shrank to 9 percent while those wearing blue collars only dropped to 18 percent. At 45 and above, the two groups resumed roughly the same percentages of the discontented. These shifts reflect, one suspects, the economic squeeze blue-collar workers face in middle life. As former Assistant Secretary of Labor Jerome M. Rosow reminds us, blue-collar workers are more likely to achieve top earnings earlier in life than white-collar workers, who begin in their 30s to reap the rewards of greater education.

Women were considerably more likely to express discontent than men but within the same income ranges the differences between the sexes tended to disappear. This confirms the essential rightness of the feminist demand for equal pay for equal work.

Worker dissatisfaction increases slightly with greater education, stepping up a percentage point or two as the education level rises from elementary school to high school and beyond. Not surprisingly, those who progressed beyond high school tended to be unhappier than workers with less education in the same income bracket, whether that bracket was under $5,000 or between $5,000 and $10,000. When you get above $10,000 a year, seemingly, your troubles slip away as you join the income group expressing the least dissatisfaction with their jobs and life.

In 1970, Sheppard, who is staff social scientist for the Upjohn Institute, went looking for "the blues" among a group of Pennsylvania and Michigan blue-collar, white, male, union members. What he found reinforces the findings of the national survey, only the percentage of workers with the blues was higher, 22 percent of Sheppard's sample as against 13 percent of the national sample. Whether or not a worker has the blues or, in more scholarly vernacular, is alienated, turns on his quotient of success or achievement. "Workers with the blues," writes Sheppard, "are the ones much more likely to (a) feel their jobs do not measure up to their original hopes; (b) believe that compared with their hopes when finished with school, they are not as well off as they hoped to be; and (c) claim that they are behind in the things they've wanted out of life, compared with where they were 10 years ago." It is interesting to note that of the workers with the blues — a minority of 22 percent remember — 53 percent stated that their current job is not very much like the one they wanted; 70 percent said it did not measure up to high school graduation hopes but only 29 percent stated that they were behind as compared to 10 years ago. Sheppard offers no explanation but my guess is that their union must have done fairly well at the bargaining table for these men.

Curiously, workers with the blues in Sheppard's study

turned out to have a far greater proportion, 45 percent, with one or more additional members of the family working than do workers without the blues, 32 percent. Clearly, this had to do with earnings; 49 percent of the workers with the blues said that their own take-home pay was not enough to take care of their family as against 27 percent of those without the blues. Their earnings were less — 37 percent reported family incomes of less than $8,000 as compared with only 30 percent of those without the blues.

Not unnaturally, 70 percent of the workers with the blues held that their jobs were without variety, autonomy and responsibility, while only 41 percent of the workers without the blues said the same about their jobs. Sociologists argue, and they are certainly correct, that a worker's perception about his job is accurate. If a worker says he has a grundgy job, he surely has. Sheppard adds that his analysis "demonstrates to my satisfaction that there is a relationship between the odds for a worker being 'blue' and the amount of variety and autonomy he perceives his job provides him."

No one, least of all a trade unionist, discounts the debilitation of a lifetime of drudgery. And I for one would not seriously quarrel with the factual findings, as limited as they are, of the various surveys of workers' discontent. But interpretations and recommendations for action are another matter. And here I confess to profound unease, for I detect an underlying contempt for working people and a scorn for their unions as well as the creation of a new myth and a new conventional wisdom.

Ignoring history and present performance, the sociologists of alienation tend to view unions as part of the establishment. For example, Robert Ardrey, a pop prophet of the new sociology, writes: "But labor unions dedicated to the cause of human mediocrity must and will oppose any change." Michael Maccoby, a behaviorial scientist and psychoanalyst, asserts, without evidence, "Probably, some union leaders would have resistances (to job enrichment or humanizing work) similar to those of the managers who are threatened by autonomous workers. The free worker is more likely to question the organization and decisions of the union as well as those of the industrial organization. As Marcus Raskin argues, the unions have bargained away the quality of work for security and benefits and have become a powerful force to keep workers 'in line'."

The new conventional wisdom also holds that young workers will not be kept in line. Young workers will not tolerate working conditions passively accepted by older workers. Starting with the kernel that in percentage terms more young workers express discontent with their jobs than do older workers, the new sociology works up an oak tree of anti-authoritarianism. Maccoby, for example, declares "younger workers are more democratic and less authoritarian. Members of the new generation are more self-affirmative and expect to be treated with respect by their employers. They seek work that allows them to be more active and autonomous." Older workers are, of course, robots, mechanistic idiots, who never talk back to their bosses and accept "the authoritarian way of doing things."

Robert N. Ford, an AT&T personnel officer and a management pioneer in the new way, puts the not-so-new attitude bluntly: "We've run out of dumb people to handle those dumb jobs. So we have to re-think what we are doing."

Much is made in radical chic academic and intellectual circles of the strike at the Lordstown, Ohio, Chevrolet Vega plant, where a predominantly young workforce struck over the speed-up, safety and other work conditions. The role of the United Auto Workers in formulating negotiable issues out of vague discontents and specific grievances was totally ignored by intellectuals and the mass media alike. From the newspapers and magazine accounts, one would think that these young workers were on strike not only against General Motors but chiefly against older workers and their union. Legend now has it that this strike was a part of the "youth rebellion." In fact, it was another strike in the long struggle of auto workers to improve their lot. A similar strike over like issues in Norwood, Ohio, received zero attention because it did not fit into the new conventional wisdom. The Norwood workers, you see, are older.

Young workers today are in the position of the young

lad seated on his father's shoulder to view the passing parade. He can see further than his father but this does not mean that the father is less perceptive than the son. When workers protest today's work conditions, they stand on gains won in the past. The workers at Lordstown, for example, were able to strike with some success because their union long ago won the right for auto workers to strike over local unresolved grievances.

When sociologists Robert H. Guest and Stanley H. Udy, Jr., recently looked into a "Plant X" studied some 20 years ago by Charles R. Walker and Guest, they found, "the average worker seems to view his immediate job in much the same way as workers did a generation ago. Today, as before, workers express negative attitudes toward highly fractionated job content, repetitiveness and the unrelenting mechanical pacing of the conveyor. . . . Workers holding repair jobs and other jobs with greater variety expressed less dissatisfaction than did regular line workers, with the latter aspiring to non-production jobs." A recent NBC television documentary about dissatisfied young workers portrayed a "hippie" assembly-line worker who soon followed his electrician father's footsteps, cutting his hair and becoming an apprentice. The more things change, the more they remain the same.

Union leaders are criticized for stressing pay and fringe benefits when workers, it is claimed, place a higher priority on non-economic aspects of their jobs. Workers in the Michigan national survey were asked how important they considered some 25 aspects of work, including pay, working conditions and relations with co-workers. Of the five work features rated most important, good pay was ranked fifth. Interesting work, enough help and equipment to get the job done, enough information to get the job done and enough authority to do the job were ranked above good pay in that order. Herrick and his co-workers therefore conclude: "I would suggest . . . that we take the worker at his word and seriously question our traditional notions regarding his needs and priorities."

This is indeed a crucial issue. Should unions stress job satisfaction, work fulfillment or the humanization of work above the mundane demand for more money and better fringe benefits? A ranking of fifth in a list of 25 job "aspects" is very high and certainly not low enough to warrant, by itself, a re-ordering of priorities that would place an abstract "quality of life" above the concrete "quantity in the pay packet." By comparing what workers considered "very important" job criteria and the extent each one was present on the job, the Michigan pollsters established a job satisfaction index. And, lo and behold, the second largest satisfaction gap was "good pay," with "promotional opportunity" the largest. But more workers gave a very important rating to good pay than to promotions, by 64 percent to 55 percent. The gap was created because 25 percent reported good chances of promotion as a characteristic of their job while 40 percent declared that they enjoyed good pay. The third largest satisfaction gap was "opportunity to develop one's special abilities," with "adequacy of fringe benefits" fourth and "interesting work" fifth.

No one denies that there are boring jobs, dead-end jobs, dirty jobs, jobs where the machine operates the worker. Why else do workers unionize but to do something about their condition? The issue is not what ought to be done but what can be done; how and by whom.

Management talks of job enrichment and the sociologists of participatory democracy in the workplace. Both tend to overlook the unions. In the case of management, that attitude is understandable, even predictable. In the case of the sociologists, it is instructive to observe how they work. For instance, one would think that having found a group of satisfied workers — such as in construction, where only one in 20 workers is reportedly dissatisfied — the sociologists would examine the experiences of construction craftsmen to see if anything might be learned for application elsewhere. But no, they invariably turn to a handful of experiments being conducted by management among non-union workers. Are they put off, one wonders, by the fact that the construction worker's pride in his craft and his autonomy is firmly rooted in ownership of his tools, through which he symbolically owns his job and controls his destiny — with all of it protected by his union? Might they find, in other words, that all they desire for workers is created by the worker through his union?

Several years back I had occasion to write an article about participatory management for *Dun's Review* and I was immediately struck by three facts: the experimenting firms were all small, of a flexible technology and non-union. Fred K. Foulkes of the Harvard business administration school recently reported that only a few companies — 40 or 50 — have implemented work improvement principles and were for the most part non-union firms. Many such experiments were in new plants. Notable experiments, for example, have been carried out by General Foods in Kansas, Olin and Procter and Gamble plants in Georgia and Corning Glass and Polaroid facilities in Massachusetts. Each new plant is conceived of as both a social and technological system, in which those involved in operating the plant participate as early as possible in the design and development of the new facility, share in the determination of work arrangements, the content of individual jobs and the development of personnel and compensation policies. Other gimmicks or features include dispensing with time clocks, developing work teams, meetings for "goal setting" and an extensive exchange of information. Jobs are designed "to maximize personal involvement" and "organization cohesiveness." And always at hand, one finds the consultant skilled in group dynamics and organizational developments. "These companies," says Foulkes, "view these plants as experiments in management. . . ." And, he adds, non-union companies see the new techniques "as a way to stay unorganized."

This is not to say that unions have nothing to learn from these "experiments." For one thing, they do demonstrate that small groups of workers can be granted large amounts of autonomy. Workers, as we all know, exercise an informal discipline which can be counted on to get the work done under circumstances determined by the workers themselves. The division of labor can be carried to a point of no return. In some industries, electronics for example, units may be assembled by individual workers more profitably than putting them together piece by piece on an assembly line. And in automated, continuous-flow industries like oil refining, job rotation is more rewarding than keeping a worker glued to a particular pipe line, valve or vat. Even that traditional assembly line, the automobile industry, is amenable to change.

In Sweden, for example, auto workers in new plants assemble the whole engine and, where production lines cannot be changed, the individual worker may follow the car along performing a variety of tasks instead of simply turning the same bolt day in and day out. Groups of workers determine who will do what and elect team leaders to replace the traditional foreman. In this country, Chrysler Corporation is experimenting with self-supervision and encouraging workers to take short-cuts in getting out the work. In some situations, workers can take a day off without questions asked so long as they give prior notice.

Dumping green workers on the line without preparation has been a source of difficulty. I once had a young Dodge worker, smarting from a punishment meted out for absenteeism, tell me, "In a place that big, you wouldn't think that they would miss me!" General Motors and Chrysler in a number of plants are experimenting with a new worker orientation plan whereby both union and company representatives spend a day informing newcomers of their rights and obligations.

Contrary to what the new ideologists of job enrichment and humanizing work say, trade unions are very much a part of the workers' own efforts to make work more tolerable if not fully enjoyable. But their efforts were — and are — circumscribed, to put it politely, by management and the limits of industrial production. The machine is in place before the worker is hired; he is not consulted about its design or use. Indeed, this is the classic difference between the craftsman, who owns his tools and has a good deal to say through his union about their use, in contrast with the factory worker. This fact of industrial life is what made the period of the late 1950's so crucial in labor history. For the first time, as management automated and re-tooled on a large scale, factory workers had an opportunity to affect the very fundamentals of their jobs. Unions called for advance consultation whenever employees planned major job changes, job transfers and retraining rights, negotiation of new job classifications and a more equitable distribution of the gains resulting from greater productivity. These issues go to the very heart of the alienation and blue-collar blues now being studied so assiduously by a new generation of industrial sociologists and psychologists.

Workers have had generations of experience with management wielding stopwatches. The impetus for time-and-motion studies is pretty much the same as that behind job enrichment or participatory management. Substituting the sociologist's questionnaire for the stopwatch is likely to be no gain for the workers. While workers have a stake in productivity it is not always identical with that of management. Job enrichment programs have cut jobs just as effectively as automation or engineers' stopwatches. And the rewards of productivity are not always equitably shared.

Workers' participation or job enrichment without union involvement is apt to be an illusion. Management, after all, as Polaroid did in one instance, can cancel its "experiments" at will should they prove unprofitable. Collective bargaining gives working men and women some say about the condition of their employment. No other technique of job enrichment has done as much. Beyond this fundamental, however, I also find profoundly disturbing the ready acceptance of the unjustifiable conclusion that satisfied workers are proponents of the status quo, against change and conservative. In one academic study, for example, workers who voted for Hubert H. Humphrey are seen as authoritarian while those who voted for George Wallace are anti-authoritarian.

Undoubtedly, hard-hats are "in," but fashion brings Archie Bunker spouting his prejudices, which are passed off as typical working class wisdom. The truth is, the bulk of the working class is a force for social stability and for economic advance and socially conscious legislative gains. Workers do not want change for change's sake but they do want progress — a much abused concept.

Much of what is passed off as new in the current surveys of worker dissatisfaction is an updating of the findings of Elton Mayo of Harvard, a pioneer in industrial research, and succeeding schools of industrial sociology. I am, therefore, encouraged by a story I heard when I first began studying labor history. During the late 1940s, a major manufacturer built a new plant and drawing upon Mayo, installed the equivalent of Musak and dining facilities and also restructured the work, cossetted the workers in the approved way and the like. Pay and fringe benefits were on par with other employment in the area. When union organizers showed up at the plant gate, they made little headway. Finally, an organizer had a brilliant idea, he passed out a leaflet saying, "Do You Want to be a Guinea Pig or a Man?" The workers, by 100 percent, went union.

Job Satisfaction II: Sorting Out the Nonsense

by William Gomberg

In the Michigan Survey Research Center study, Neal Herrick of the U. S. Department of Labor, closely associated with the project, noted 25 aspects of work in which inquiry was made. The eight aspects of work receiving top ranking in importance follow in the sequence in which the results were arranged: interesting work; enough equipment and help to get the job done; enough information; enough authority; good pay; opportunity to develop special abilities; job security; and seeing the result of one's work.

Implying that trade unions are wont to concentrate exclusively on pay and job security, Herrick suggests that "we take the worker at his word and seriously question traditional notions regarding his needs and priorities."

This summation has been used by a widely assorted collection of behavioral scientists to conclude that the worker is concerned beyond all else with the nature of his work, the actual job description, constrained by a technology that is assumed to be fixed and that this source of frustration has been completely neglected by the trade unions, which have confined themselves to the problems of job security and job pay.

In another lengthy document, *Work in America*, they offer their services to overcome these problems: they suggest the formation of a public corporation with the following kinds of functions:

1. To compile and certify a roster of qualified consultants

Reprinted with permission from the *AFL-CIO American Federationist*, June 1973.

to assist employees with the technical problems in altering
work.

2. To provide a resource to which management and labor can turn for advice and assistance.

3. To provide an environment in which researchers from
various disciplines who are working on job redesign can meet
with employers, unions and workers to pool their experiences and findings.

Work in America was prepared by a 10-man task force,
headed by James O'Toole, a social anthropologist, for the U. S.
Department of Health, Education and Welfare.

A review of these documents, their analysis of what ails
the American workers, their knowledge of the role of unions
in responding to workers' needs and their wants, their philosophy of past experimentation and present remedial prescriptions are long overdue.

Mitchell Fein, an industrial engineer, questions the findings of the Michigan Survey Group. He notes that they have
used the term "worker" to encompass managers, professionals,
and the like as well as the conventional blue-collar worker.

The Survey Research Center data was reworked by Fein
to separate out the blue-collar data and he found that pay,
which was fifth in the university analysis, jumped to first
place. My own feeling is that these first eight work aspects
may be listed in most any manner. Fein could have spared
himself the effort. The number of measurement points sep-
arating these characteristics is so minute that any ranking is
arbitrary — they are virtually all of equal weight. The important consideration is that Herrick's conclusion betrays
a superficial knowledge of what collective bargaining is all
about.

The general public, when it reads about collective bargaining, confines its attention to wages. The professional un-
derstands that the myriad of working conditions, out of which
virtually all arguments arise during the course of the administration of the contract, are closely tied to the remaining seven
aspects of work that head the Survey Research Center list.
Grievances over promotions, lack of equipment to do the job
right, lack of help and information to do the job right dom-

inate the grievance procedure. They are the warp and woof of daily collective bargaining.

The HEW document on work observes that all of the problems of modern job design are attributable to Frederick W. Taylor, who is accused of fractionating work and making the worker an extension of the machine with the implicit, supine consent of the labor movement.

This must be news to many unions, including the Machinists, which has had a long history of conflict in this area early in this century. And it perhaps explains the impatience of Machinists Vice President William W. Winpisinger, who has pointed out that just as job dissatisfaction in the workplace yielded to trade union solutions in the past, such dissatisfaction can be decreased to the extent that trade union solutions are applied today.

As a case in hand, Winpisinger says that "perhaps when workers first negotiated the right to bid on better shifts, overtime and promotions on the basis of length of service, they weren't thinking in terms of 'job enrichment,' but in actual practice that's what they got."

There are deep roots to Winpisinger's thinking. In 1912, a young professor, Robert Franklin Hoxie of the University of Chicago, was retained by John R. Commons of the University of Wisconsin, who had undertaken an investigation of the scientific management movement on behalf of Congress. In the manuscript published in 1915, *Scientific Management and Labor,* Hoxie listed the objections of the labor movement to scientific management. The Machinists union was then in the forefront of the federation's struggle with this innovation. With the machinists in the vanguard, the trade unionists indicted the new technique on the grounds that it:

— tends to deprive the worker of thought, initiative, achievement and joy in his work;

— tends to eliminate skilled crafts;

— is destructive of mechanical education and skill;

— tends to deprive the worker of the possibility of learning a trade;

— condemns the worker to a monotonous routine;

— dwarfs and represses the worker intellectually;

— tends to destroy the individuality and inventive genius of the workers;

— stimulates and drives the workers up to the limits of nervous and physical exhaustion and over-fatigues and over-strains them;

— tends to reduce the workers to complete dependence on the employer — to the condition of industrial serfs.

"Most significant of all, scientific management puts into the hands of employers at large an immense mass of information and methods which may be used unscrupulously to the detriment of the workers and offers no guarantee against the abuse of its professed principles and practices. And most important of all, it forces the workers to depend upon the employers' conception of fairness and limits the democratic safeguards of the workers!"

Now for a trade union group which was fighting back in 1915 to be told now that it is reactionary invokes some justifiable impatience with job enrichment experts who are now attempting to reverse the alleged handicaps of job fractionation.

For many years the labor movement was at complete loggerheads with the scientific management movement. No small part of the reason for that conflict was the personality of Frederick W. Taylor himself. His autocratic ways hardly endeared him to the members of the labor movement. However, in 1919 Samuel Gompers, meeting together with Morris L. Cook, an engineer who understood the principles of democracy, established a new relationship between the scientific management movement and the trade unionists.

Morris L. Cook co-authored a book with Philip Murray in 1940 called *Organized Labor and Production* in which were laid down the fundamental principles of the participative management movement that is now being rediscovered by the sociologists. This volume was founded upon a set of principles laid down by Robert G. Valentine, a Boston social worker turned management expert, in a famous paper in 1916, "The Relationship Between Efficiency and Consent." This principle was stated as follows: "The organization of workers can be counted on to consent to all that makes for efficiency under constitutional industrial relations. They will contest the share in the management and share of the product between themselves and the consumer. For the most part, the labor agreements in operation today are looked upon by employers as a necessary evil and by the workers as steps in their reassertion of rights as consumers and having little detailed relation to production processes. The beginning of something far better than this is seen in the agreements in the garment trades wherein the manufacturers, the workers and the public are all represented as parties."

The division of labor does not date from Frederick W. Taylor — it goes back to Adam Smith, who wrote in the *Wealth of Nations* in 1776: "This great increase of the quantity of work which in consequence of the division of labor, the same number of people are capable of performing, is owing to three different circumstances: first, to the increase of dexterity in every particular workman; secondly, to the saving of the time which is commonly lost in passing from one species of work to another; and lastly, to the invention of a great number of machines which facilitate one man to do the work of many."

Adam Smith, when he wrote these lines, was as aware as the modern behavioralist that what specialization did to the worker as a human exacted a social cost — the "externalities" as they are called by the modern economist. Those costs shifted by the management to others because the price does not appear in conventional accounting systems have been a subject over which trade unionists have mulled long before they were formalized by economists and ecologists.

The labor movement has spent no small part of its energy in reassigning the cost of externalities so that they no longer fall exclusively on the workers. They have pioneered sickness, health and pension programs to lighten his burden. Labor's lobby has put legislation on the books requiring the observance of a safety code in the 1970 Occupational Safety and Health Act that is unprecedented.

It, too, is aware that the division of labor, like many

another phenomenon, can be carried so far that it reaches a point of diminishing returns. It is also aware that the re-unification of work can be carried so far that we will have happy workers producing for customers who have been priced out of the market. Reaching an intelligent balance is an occasion for rational analysis rather than evangelistic preaching.

All workers are not the same. Many workers will take advantage of the undemanding nature of their market-oriented work to engage in reverie or in thinking about things of more importance to them than their work. The worker may find his or her primary source of satisfaction in the after hours living that his or her market-oriented work provides so that he or she is able to do what he or she is really interested in during leisure hours. When the jobs of these workers are enriched, very often the monotony of 15 repetitive jobs instead of the monotony of one job becomes a source of distraction rather than satisfaction.

The labor movement has endeavored in the past to provide opportunities to management who were seeking higher production and its members who were seeking more challenging work. Labor history is replete with labor-management experiments like the Baltimore and Ohio plan on the railroads from 1926 to the depression in which workers were able to show management aspects of management's task that the latter had overlooked.

This is only one of a long line of historic undertakings. As late as 1960 the Kaiser Steel Long Range Union-Management Plan displayed how creative workers could be who were technically oriented and were given a chance to participate jointly in the cost savings. The rediscovery of participative management by the behaviorists in the last few years is more an invention of vocabulary than occupational technique.

The trade unionists have probably done more to eliminate sub-human work by raising wages than all of the elaborate schemes of the scholars laid end to end. When employers find that they must pay high wages for what they consider sub-human, repetitive work they somehow manage to automate the job so that it is no longer performed by a human.

In fact, the higher the wage, the more likely the employer is to seek a capital substitute for the worker. For example, suppose an international road building contractor owns a trench digging machine that does the work of 100 men. He owns only one of these machines and he has contracts to dig ditches in Taiwan and in New York City. Where is he likely to use the machine? Obviously in New York City where the rate for common labor, protected by unions, is quite high rather than in Taiwan where a few cents an hour additional expended by employing more labor spares the employer the risk of investing in a machine.

All of the claims being made for the miraculous increases in productivity and worker satisfaction by the evangelistic behaviorists have been heard before.

Back in the 1930s a management consultant, Allan Mogensen, founded the work simplification movement. He was training workers and management in participative techniques. Workers were indoctrinated with a set of motion principles to apply to their various jobs. They took great joy in using their ingenuity to fractionate their jobs and other jobs with the same miraculous reports of increased productivity that we now get from the behaviorist for doing the opposite of the work simplification experts. This former enthusiasm ran its course.

In fact, behaviorists have invented a name for these spurts in productivity that seem to come with any kind of initial attention to long-neglected workers. They call it "the Hawthorne effect" after the pioneering experiments at the Hawthorne plant of the Bell System in Chicago in the 1930s. A proper test calls for an extended longitudinal study of many of these modifications to see if they are real. Too often the initial spurt is followed by a return to "normal."

Of interest is Fein's analysis of the much publicized General Food-Pet Food case in Topeka, Kansas, which is a nonunion operation. Basically, what is claimed is that it was an innovative experiment in rescuing and revamping a low-morale workforce. But it really was a matter of running away from the original problems, in an Illinois plant, and building an ideal work environment through a careful selection of new personnel and the advantages of new physical facilities in Kansas.

"In discussing the General Food-Pet case, the HEW task force shows its myopia and bias toward the problems in plants which affect management and workers," Fein says. "Typical is their description of why General Foods management decided to build a new plant at Topeka: 'Management built this plant because the employes in an existing plant manifested many severe symptoms of alienation. Because of their indifference and inattention, the continuous process type of technology used in the plant was susceptible to frequent shutdowns, to product waste and to costly recycling. There were serious acts of sabotage and violence. Employes worked effectively for only a few hours a day and strongly resisted changes that would have resulted in a further utilization of manpower.'

"This statement sounds as if it were written by the PR department of a company which was preparing a public case for abandoning its old plant.

"What was not reported . . . was the strategy for hiring employes for the new plant. This is described by L. D. Ketchum, Manager of Organization Development Operations at G-F. An ad was run in the local press:

" 'General Foods — Topeka plant needs production people: Work in a new, modern Gaines Pet Food Plant with an exciting new organization concept which will allow you to participate in all phases of plant operations.

" 'Qualifications: mechanical aptitude; willing to accept greater responsibility; willing to work rotating shifts; desire to learn multiple jobs and new skills.

" 'If you would like to work with an organization that emphasizes individual potential, learning and responsibility, with excellent earnings and benefits, job interviews will be conducted. . . .' "

The hiring process proceeded as follows, according to Fein's description: 625 people applied. (Other reports say over 700 applied.) Screening by the State Employment Service and the team leaders eliminated 312. Many of these eliminated themselves. Testing eliminated 76, so 237 remained. The physical examination eliminated 18, and the balance went through an in-depth interview, an hour each, with three different team leaders and this eliminated 121. The team leaders then designed a selection weekend and began with 98, eliminated 35, leaving 63 who were offered jobs. King, a consultant to the program, adds that when the applicants were down to 98, they were invited to spend a Saturday at the plant for the final selections. After a one and a half hour tour of the plant, the applicants worked for two hours on a NASA problem exercise, to determine how they would react under different circumstances at work. The supervisors then selected 63 for jobs in the plant.

"The new Topeka employes were screened for special skills and profiles to match the organization criteria that had been established for the new plant," Fein continues. "In a normal employe market, screening one out of four applicants is considered fairly tight. Here only one out of 10 was selected. The new Topeka employes were a special breed; they were 'non-union achievers' who preferred working in autonomous situations. They were obviously not typical of a cross-section. . . .

"Attributing the superior performance of the Topeka employes to the organization development principles completely ignores that the Topeka employes were carefully selected for the plant. . . .

"The results obtained at Topeka are valid only for Topeka. This was a stacked experiment in a small plant with conditions set up and controlled to achieve a desired result. These employes were not a cross-section of the population, or even of Topeka. The plant and its operations are not typical of those in industry today. What are the other managers to do? Screen one in 10 employes and hire only these? And what about the other nine?"

My object in citing this analysis by Fein is not to make the point that behaviorists are anti-union as a class. They are not. What is worse is that by and large, so many of them are indifferent. They are without conviction in the matter. Now such an attitude is understandable in value-free engineers, but how are we to regard evangelistic behavorial scientists converted to participative managerial democracy who have failed to understand democracy's most fundamental tenet? Democracy cannot exist where management is free to give and to take without any countervailing force. Such "democracy" makes as much sense as a U.S. government without any institutionalized checks and balances.

The behaviorists have pointed up a problem. Their lack of knowledge of labor history may have led to an exaggeration of what they have come up with. Nevertheless, the problem is real. Its solution calls not only for technical competence, but moral commitment.

It Makes No Difference Now

by Robert Schrank

"It makes no difference now," the name of a country western song, seems an appropriate description of a new attitude in the workplace — and maybe of new troubles brewing in America. We have heard from the students, the minorities, the women; now from the workforce — maybe not all 80 million but a good part of it, particularly the young. It is common to read in *The Wall Street Journal, Time* and *Newsweek* that there are lots of new problems at the workplace. What used to be referred to as alienation has turned into a much more difficult problem that I call indifference. It has management experts, industrial psychologists, and systems analysts all trying to figure out what has gone wrong. The result of the disturbance is a new virus, "lackoproduction."

Workers stay home in such numbers on Fridays and Mondays that some plants have had to shut down for lack of personnel. When employees are asked why they didn't show, they give replies like, "I had to go shopping" or "I went to pay my gas bill." Turnover rates have been steadily rising. Companies which used to be considered blue chip places to work now experience a turnover rate of as much as 50 per cent in a year on many of their best jobs. Many young people simply refuse to do the jobs they consider dirty or uncomfortable.

Companies have responded to this indifference with threats, rewards, seduction, speeches, watches, bowling, picnics — old stuff that doesn't work anymore. There are also

Reprinted with permission from *New Generation*. Copyright © 1970 by the National Committee on Employment of Youth.

some new things I will discuss later. Nobody quite knows what has happened. What is clear is that during the fifties and sixties a new kind of employee entered the workplace and changed it. Employee indifference is one of the changes I suggest we don't know much about. It resembles passive resistance. Yet, it may very well be the influence of the youth culture with its challenges to America's traditional values. This article will speculate on some of these changes and their implications.

Beginning with the Industrial Revolution, the role of the individual in production is slowly being eliminated. The goal has always been to eliminate as much individual variation in the production process as possible, first through mechanization and now through automation. As a result, emphasis and status have gradually shifted from manual to white-collar and technical work. The big change has occurred since World War II; the process has accelerated so rapidly it has run out of anyone's control. Technology seems to have simply taken over and now has a life of its own.

Employers complain, "the unemployed won't take low level jobs; nobody wants to do the dirty work." And why should they? Since technology's takeover, society has formed an invidious image of the manual worker as the one who didn't make it. The old ghetto argument that the bookie in a sport shirt, driving a Continental, is a far greater success symbol than some poor black man who has been working thirty years for $60 a week is partly based on this change.

Job specialization is another change in the production process that has accelerated tremendously since World War II. The ultimate in scientific management was an attempt to program the activities of individual workers down to the nth degree. Specialization has become so minute in many cases that a worker's time and physical activity is completely accounted for. This contribution of Taylor and his scientific management teams speeded mass production. The fact that it also increased worker alienation has been well documented.

However, the daily press accounts of employee indifference describe worker attitudes that seem to go beyond the alienation we have read and heard about for so long. The dissatisfaction which formerly was endured in relative silence now gets acted out as indifference or failure to respond to the various motivational efforts to get people to produce. What brought about the transformation?

A combination of factors are at work which affect different persons in varied degrees. I would suggest that the following are some of the most critical reasons. First, there is the new labor force. They confound personnel interviews. They don't accept traditional supervision. They are not easily threatened. They don't accept their union leadership. These are the youth who have gone to work in the last decade. They are bringing their youth culture to the workplace. They have more years of schooling. They have grown up on television and the credibility gap. They are less authoritarian than their fathers. Most of all, they do not seem anxious about job security.

Second, our society is basically future oriented — we have no dusty historical tradition behind us. We tend to derive our status more from present life style and future potential than from past accomplishments. Thus, most American workers evaluate their jobs in terms of the future. As more and more blue-collar work is automated, the future looks dimmer and dimmer for manual workers. The myth and reality of the computer age — automation, cybernetics, etc. — convince many workers that their jobs will be eliminated. This is a sure-fire way to cut down a man's motivation. In the same way that he lets a car run down when he knows he'll replace it next year, the man lets down his involvement with his job, if he believes he'll be replaced.

Third, for over twenty-five years, a large segment of American society has lived in affluence. Many of the 1970's workforce know little about the anxieties of layoffs, depressions and unemployment. The young, especially, have a very relaxed attitude about finding and holding a job. When people are not full of anxiety over job security, they are free to move to a higher level of needs. I see the new indifference as an expression of the desire for satisfactions in work that go beyond having a job and making a living. As S. M. Miller puts it, people in the 1970's are more and more concerned with the quality of life; they are less and less satisfied with meaningless work activity. The new indifference is but the first silent, almost unconscious, expression of this new desire for quality in one's life.

Fourth, the media have brought the world into everyman's living room. They tell him how he ought to live. They have bombarded him with status symbols to the point where the symbols become all important. Television creates a World Series of who is making it and who isn't. It shows white-collar people as the only decision makers. Television accentuates many workers' feeling of being "out of it" by dramatizing the strong advocacy roles taken by students, peaceniks, civil rights demonstrators and others. The unions, which formerly made big noises on behalf of their members, have not maintained a strong advocacy position. They have generally become institutionalized and conservative. Many workers see other groups in the limelight and no one out there fighting for the blue-collar man. This reinforces their sense of blue-collar demise.

Fifth, there is a whole new range of white-collar jobs that the blue-collar man sees as non-work. This aggravates his non-motivation. There are white-collar jobs in which people appear to do little actual work and still be reasonably well paid. A man who sits and watches a monitor board and periodically pushes a button is a non-worker in the eyes of a machine operator or an assembly line man. The issue of what is work becomes sharpened as white-collar jobs steadily increase. Society seems to be caught between a lag in the Post-industrial Revolution for some workers and advancing technology for others. Implicit in this dislocation is conflict between those involved in the old technologies and those involved with the new.

Sixth, the educational level of the work force is rising steadily. Today's worker is better educated (12.2 years median in 1968 vs. 10.0 in 1958), more sophisticated, and therefore has higher aspirations. The new worker is most likely to demand far more opportunity for personal expression and socialization in the workplace. He does not see his life compartmentalized between the job, which is a drag, and living, which takes place after five o'clock. Increased education has contributed to greater expectations. In that sense, education, with all the criticism made of it, becomes a real force for change. In fact, there seems to be a growing correlation between educational level and worker expectation. The more education, the less willingness to put up with the repetitive, meaningless, boring, minute task-repetition associated with most production lines.

Because of the inflexible nature of the production line, white-collar jobs usually allow more freedom than blue-collar work. Coffee breaks, conversations formal and informal, conferences, seminars, personal and business meetings, gossip, and wasting time all break up the day. The physical setting is clean. You wear clean clothes; you come and go without having to change your appearance significantly. Finally, you are free to socialize with co-workers; there is at least a minimum sense of community. This need for community is one of the new youth factors pushing for change in the workplace.

Despite these positive factors and the prestige attached to white-collar work, many white-collar workers are showing signs of discontent. Many also complain of "meaninglessness." While the white-collar workplace is clean and comfortable, the growing sense of indifference may be coming from the same tendency to overspecialize job functions that created the problems on the production floor.

Management's attempts to deal with employee indifference range over a variety of schemes which fall into several categories. The first consists of what Herzberg calls the hygiene factors of wages, hours, and working conditions. Interestingly enough, these factors seem to be less important for the new work force. Hence the impatience of the young with the unions, since this is their primary turf. The second consists of changes in the job itself, usually referred to as job enrichment and job redesign. The third involves efforts to change the employee through sensitivity training, seminars, and after hours educational courses. In the last two areas, management is trying to introduce personal variation and socialization to the workplace under controllable conditions.

Changes in the job itself usually focus on the indifference of the workforce. When the indifference threatens corporate efficiency, management may accept the fact that much of the work is routine, requires little or no judgment, and is oppressive. Highly developed skills may be involved in the overall product but overspecialization has so fragmented the tasks that there are few, if any, chances for individuality. The worker's sense of depersonalization is heightened by status inequities between himself and salaried white-collar workers.

The new technocraftsman who manages a logic-controlled machine may work very close to the production worker. This view of the future worker, operating in an air-conditioned control room in his white shirt, is visual evidence to the blue-collar worker that the production line job is going nowhere. It is part of our American value system that we need to have a sense of going somewhere.

Job changes addressed to these complaints involve easing many company practices that traditionally separate white- and blue-collar workers. They are designed to help the blue-collar worker put up with the routine nature of his work by letting him identify with the white-collar staff. *Fortune* (September, 1970) described the steps currently being taken in this direction by a few companies: cutting out special dining rooms and parking privileges, removal of time clocks, ending hourly pay, etc. This final item seems particularly popular with blue-collar employees, many of whom resent the tight control that a time clock and hourly pay exercise. Many other "white-collar benefits," such as vacations, health and education programs, pensions, etc., have long been opened to blue-collars. Removal of hourly wage rates is a further step in a continuing process.

Management is also trying to deal with the new workers' demand for an end to isolation and the desire for community. The organization of worker teams in a variety of tasks is one attempt to deal with isolation. The telephone company has used this scheme in several of its job redesign efforts. Often, the teams are made responsible for accomplishing a whole unit of production rather than giving each individual separate tasks in isolation from one another. The camaraderie that develops in these teams helps to create a sense of community and decreases the worker's isolation to compensate for the routine nature of the work.

Job rotation is another management technique for dealing with indifference. In these programs workers move among several jobs on a regular schedule. They acquire new skills and perform a variety of tasks within a day, week or month. This does not answer their socialization and community needs but eases some of the monotony of repetitive tasks. It is assumed that the feeling of personal responsibility for a unit of work, rather than a single task, increases the individual's job interest.

These job enrichment and rotation schemes seem to have had some success in reducing the indifference expressed in turnover and absences. Product quality has also improved, indicating greater worker interest. These programs have not been applied on a broad enough scale to make any overall evaluation. Where they have been tried, they do seem to make the workplace more tolerable.

Participatory management has been a popular slogan with corporation people for some time. Its underlying assumption is that, if people participate in the decision-making process, they will be motivated to carry out the decisions. In the United States, it has been aimed primarily at management personnel from first line supervisors up. A few companies have begun to experiment with involving production workers in the making of decisions. American unions have shown little interest in this problem. Some union leaders see it as an attempt at "company unionism." This may be an extremely narrow view of a real membership issue. Traditionally American unions have accepted the view that management runs the plant. The new worker is not accepting that notion so easily. He may be closer to the Nader view that corporations are responsible to the public interest and not simply to profits.

Efforts at participatory management have generally been

aimed at reducing employee complaints about arbitrary schedules and quotas. Worker committees set quotas, evaluate progress, reassign priorities and help in other management decisions. In these participatory programs, there is wide variation
in the authority delegated to workers. Some programs appear
no more revolutionary than the old suggestion box, but some
involve profit sharing and bonus plans that were formerly
white-collar turf. I don't think too much can be accomplished
with participatory management schemes without union co-
operation. Hopefully, the unions will begin to respond to
their young members' interest in changing the nature of the
workplace. The militant tradition of the union is of little or
no interest to the new member. He simply has trouble understanding how a man can spend his life putting a bumper on
a Buick.

The other broad area of management concern in the
workplace is with the individual rather than the job. Sensitivity training, encounter and t-groups, and interface have
gained widespread acceptance. These techniques are most
often aimed at supervisory and white-collar workers but are
occasionally found in blue-collar situations as well. They are
based on the assumption that people feel estranged and do
not sense themselves part of the company. The objective
seems to be to get employees emotionally and physically involved with each other and the company. The technique and
styles of the sessions vary; some encourage shouting, crying,
anger, criticism, hostility, sweat, tears, hugging, etc., as evidence of "real" interaction. If a group member hits another
or screams some insult at him, it seems to satisfy those who
feel their environment is barren. The workplace is being enriched by the introduction of the senses and of "feeling" in
an attempt to humanize it and develop a feeling of community.

There is some evidence that sensitivity type sessions are
helpful, not so much in changing behavior, but in providing
the sense of community. People who have participated often
say that they got to know people they have worked with for
years who had been total strangers and that this helped them
gain self-insight. The programs seem to satisfy many people's

needs for inter-personal exchange at work. Companies hiring large numbers of the "hard-core unemployed" and minority groups have used the sensitivity approach in preparing supervisors and the new employees for what will occur in the workplace. Industry acknowledges that these youth will not accept old style authoritarianism. Role playing, videotaped interviews, and language exercises seem to decrease the anxiety of those directly involved in these personnel changes.

Another people-oriented program sponsored by a growing number of companies is continuing education. These usually involve paid time off and/or tuition reimbursement for educational courses related to the job. Advocates of these programs believe that education broadens the "whole man," grooms him for a higher level job, or prepares him better for his present slot. In any case, they are expected to lead to more contentment and, therefore, to greater efficiency.

Most of the "worker indifference" programs appear to focus on three human needs: creativity, socialization, and status. These needs the traditional worker was willing to suppress. The youth coming to work now is unwilling to sublimate meaningful activity to his leisure time. He will not accept the schizophrenic existence of his father. He looks forward to making his life meaningful, once the basic needs of maintenance, safety, etc., are met. The major obstacle to meeting these needs is that the technical society works against creativity and "humanity." Its efficient operation depends on predictability, routinization, and conformity — anathema to the youth culture.

What does this demand in terms of changes in the workplace? Where very routine and repetitive work is involved, it may mean arranging jobs so that men and women may hold two jobs at different locations. The jobs may even involve different kinds of work. This would mean new types of scheduling for most employers.

Shifts in working hours offer another way to lessen the strain of routine work and allow for more creativity and socialization. This is a good example of why unions should be involved, since work hours is a normal part of collective bargaining. Some small firms have already experimented with a nine- or ten-hour per day, four-day work week. Their experience suggests that for certain types of firms, the sacred eight-hour day and five-day week should be re-examined. Three-day weekends may be more important to some people than the sacredness of the eight-hour day. One small company which recently switched over to a four-day week improved worker productivity 15 per cent, decreased absenteeism from 7 per cent to zero and now has high employee morale and a long waiting list of applicants. Another firm has reduced absenteeism by almost 90 per cent.

Management may also have to provide more time off for employees; people find it increasingly difficult to take care of personal affairs in the time they now have. The increasing complexity of caring for personal business — getting the car fixed, visiting the doctor or waiting for a repair man — means that employees often cannot take care of these necessities.

The new worker is demanding that the work place be organized for his convenience as well as management's or don't expect him in on Friday. While all of this is disturbing to many management people, it may be the only way to produce anything. Indifference may prove a greater factor for change than marching and demonstrating.

The other major corporate accommodation is for companies to invest in the continuing education of their employees. They will do this to satisfy both the company's need for up-to-date skills and the employees' demand for upgrading and learning. The approximately 35 million persons now engaged in adult education outside the accredited educational core testify to a growing need for a change in management attitudes. Some large companies such as A.T. & T. already offer broad education reimbursement to their employees for accredited and non-accredited courses.

The U.A.W. has taken this education demand a step further in current collective bargaining. The union is asking the big three auto manufacturers for one-fourth of a cent per hour per employee for training and education. The "training and education fund" thus created is intended to be applied more broadly than the closely job-related scholarship fund the union has run in the past. This may well create new opportunities for blue-collar workers to continue their education. The contributions from the three auto companies should generate approximately five to six million dollars a year, a sizeable sum of money. Hopefully, it will be used imaginatively. The proposal as submitted to General Motors is written broadly enough so that it does not have to be just another "increase your welding skill" program.

Two good examples of the possible impact of continuing education on workers' lives are the Minority Leadership Training Program at Berkeley and the Cornell Labor Liberal Arts Program in New York City. The Berkeley program involves twenty-three minority trade unionists who came out of plants in the Bay area to the Berkeley campus to study economics, poverty, labor history, etc. These people have lived through a real learning experience which has opened hundreds of new windows to the world for them. They have the excitement of discovery about them that will tremendously enrich their lives.

The Cornell program is held in the evening. Its student body of over 250 is made up of mostly trade unionists and some community people. Students are exposed to a spectrum of subject matter ranging from general science to grievance arbitration procedures. After two years, the student body has now launched a campaign for an accredited Labor College in New York. These students, like the Berkeley group, now have a taste of learning. Their determination to expand it demonstrates that it can be like a taste of honey. That's what education is supposed to be about.

Along with the expansion of these new collective bargaining educational systems, we need to develop a method for students to accumulate educational credit over their lifetime. We recognize that jobs today require ongoing education; that people often change jobs and return to school for brush-up or advanced courses; that man's need for creativity and challenge often finds an outlet in the educational experience. Therefore, we need to provide for successive forays into the education system. The traditional method of accumulating sequential credit toward a degree in preparation for future jobs seems today to be outmoded for our fast moving society. Education should no longer be regarded as a preparatory step; it should be a continuing process. Every citizen ought to be able to have a vested education fund for his lifetime. He ought to use it as he wishes, either sequentially or intermittently. This would create second, third and fourth chances for going to school. A person would use his vested educational fund to pay for this continuing education.

There should be established a national education credit bank. This would record student achievement throughout a person's lifetime. As certain levels of credit are reached, the accrediting institution could issue degrees. Currently non-accredited courses could be evaluated and rated for credit or national exams could be established so that credentialing would no longer be the purview of traditional scholastic institutions. Such a plan would go far to assist the millions of adult learners, many of whom now take very advanced courses and receive no credit. They could eventually become credentialed. The Council of Higher Education, the National Education Association or some other national education body could take on the responsibility.

The new worker is clearly making himself felt in the workplace. He is challenging some of the sacred cows of management. It is either scary or refreshing, depending on your point of view. Clearly, there are people who are dreaming about the good old days when everyone simply did as he was told. The new worker is dislocating much of the old authoritarianism — which may be the best thing that has happened to us in a long time.

Productivity and the Blue-Collar Worker

by Jerome M. Rosow

There is a gap between productivity goals and results. But the fault is to be found more in our current inability to structure the reward system to meet new needs and requirements than in any new unwillingness to work. And if we cannot achieve further productivity gains through existing technology, it may be because we haven't looked for help to those who know the situation best: the men and women who work on the machines.

The U.S. Department of Labor has spent a great deal of time studying these workers and their problems. What we found bears directly on the problem of productivity and motivation. Millions of workers, who earn between $5,000 and $10,000 a year, are increasingly frustrated. Despite steady labor they cannot attain the quality of life for themselves or their families that is expected to result from conscientious job performance:

- Their paychecks do not cover legitimate basic family needs.
- Their work life is unsatisfactory but they see no way of breaking out.
- Their total life pattern is discouraging.

In short, they are caught in a three-way squeeze: an economic squeeze, a workplace squeeze and a socio-environmental squeeze.

These squeezes involve persons who are members of families where income is above the poverty line but below what

Reprinted with permission from *Personnel Administration*. Copyright © 1971 by The Society for Personnel Administration.

is required to meet moderate family budget needs. We estimate that some 20 million families — about 80 million individuals — are in this income range. Many are permanently trapped.

Millions of workers share in the Nation's abundance but this should not diminish concern for the other millions of steady workers who face some very basic problems.

The majority are white, but the group has a disproportionate number of nonwhites. Most of the heads of these families are blue collar workers but many are in white collar or service jobs. More are low-skilled than highly skilled, and proportionately more are non-union than union.

We are concerned about these people: lower-middle income; looking toward and aspiring to a middle-class life but achieving at best a low-quality substitute.

Let's look at the economic squeeze: This bind results from an imbalance between wages and budget-needs, aggravated by heavy taxes and inflation. In fact, inflation has eroded most of the wage increases won through collective bargaining since 1965.

Take, for example, the 40-year-old worker. He is likely to be supporting a wife and two children, one in high school. Ten years earlier he had a wife and one pre-school-age child. According to studies of the Bureau of Labor Statistics, to maintain the same standard of living for his growing family that he and his smaller family used to enjoy, he must increase his real income by about 6 percent a year.

But average productivity increases run about 3 percent a year. Over the past decade he has lost position in the economic race. And promotion opportunities and supplemental earning routes are limited:

- Promotion opportunities are restricted by mobility patterns within firms; lack of information about better jobs in other firms and inadequate educational qualifications.
- Moonlighting is limited by the availability of jobs, the physical stamina of the individual and his willingness to give up leisure time and family activities. Despite these drawbacks, at least 15 percent of lower-middle-income men moonlight.

— The scarcity of reliable, reasonably priced facilities for day care and after school supervision makes working and earning supplemental income an uphill effort for many wives. Despite a myriad of problems — including inadequate tax deductions for child care — wives in the $5-$10 thousand group work more frequently than other wives. And more than one-half of those who work have school-age children. We also have new findings which reveal that men with working wives are more alienated than other workers.

The difficulties of the 40-year-old worker may be compounded later in life when he must pay college costs and/or help support aging parents. At that point, when family budget costs are at their peak, the worker usually has reached a plateau in his job level.

The result is that after years of vigorous, dependable job performance, many find themselves *worse off* economically than when they started their working lives. This is a sad situation — in stark contrast to the American dream of rising expectations.

The problems of the worker in the lower-middle-income bracket are not confined to economics: the conditions under which he works are often less than satisfactory. Traditionally, the blue collar worker in the lower-middle-income bracket has been lower on the job satisfaction scale than a white collar worker in the same income bracket. According to studies used by *Fortune* magazine job satisfaction of white collar workers is also deteriorating.

The survey of workingmen by the University of Michigan Survey Research Center found that American workers generally expect that working entitles them to more than a paycheck; that the lack of these extras is a source of worker concern; and that millions of workers — primarily in lower-income categories — are *not* in jobs where employers provide such benefits as medical, surgical or hospital insurance, life insurance, retirement, or, for women workers, maternity leave.

The survey found that among all workers:

— 28 percent did not receive medical, surgical or hospital insurance coverage.

— 38 percent are not covered by a life insurance policy.
— 39 percent are not included in a retirement program.
— 41 percent of the women workers are not entitled to maternity leave with full reemployment rights.
— 61 percent did not have employer-sponsored training available.

The three top job-related problems, as ranked by the workers, were health and safety hazards, inadequate fringe benefits and inadequate income.

Job challenge or "interesting work" was rated by workers as *the single most important* aspect of job satisfaction. Repetitive tasks that restrict personal freedom and limit decision-making are at the root of much of the feelings of alienation. Yet that is the nature of lower-middle-income jobs.

The Michigan survey found that promotion opportunities are strongly related to job satisfaction and mental health. Workers' perceptions of the "fairness" of the promotions at their place of employment had some of the most sizable and most consistent relationships with job satisfaction/mental health measures. On each of the measures, the least favorable scores were those of workers who reported that their employers did not handle promotions fairly.

It can be assumed, because of employers' promotion-patterns for non-supervisory workers, that lack of promotion opportunities are a major source of dissatisfaction among workers in the lower-middle-income group. In fact, two out of three workers indicated that they "never" expect to be promoted from their present jobs.

It is not surprising that a preponderance of lower-income workers in the Michigan survey cited unpleasant working conditions as their major job problem: A $5,000 to $10,000 worker is much more vulnerable to boredom and repetition than is the man in a higher-income bracket.

An in-depth study of auto workers found that mental health varies consistently with the level of jobs held. Thirty percent of factory workers said they were often worried or upset, compared with 10 percent of the white collar workers. And 50 percent of repetitive production line workers felt unable to make a better future life for themselves.

Many readers are familiar with the findings of the *Fortune* magazine articles on blue collar workers: that younger workers today, much more than in past generations, expect to participate in the decision-making processes in their job-world and may turn dissatisfaction with working conditions into poor job performance and job attendance. Considering that the 25-34-year-old age group will grow by almost 50 percent in this decade, industry needs a new awareness of the younger worker. There are indications that, in contrast to former times, white collar workers also feel cut off from decision-making and any feeling of identification with the company.

Recent data from Dr. Harold Sheppard indicate that education plays a part in alienation: The highest percentage of alienation was found among older, better educated workers. This indicates that the better educated may have started out with higher aspirations than the less educated and were therefore more likely to be disappointed.

Workers in the lower-middle-income bracket are likely to live closely with some of the major environmental problems of the Nation. These combine with certain sociological and personal factors to make home life less than satisfactory:

- Off-the-job hours are likely to be spent in neighborhoods that show signs of urban decay and reduced or reducing city services, where the sense of community has been eroded by freeways and urban renewal, and where concentrations of traffic and industry intensify noise and air pollution.
- Crime and fear of crime hit hard at millions of workers, both black and white, who live in the center or near the center of the city. According to the Report of the President's Commission on the Causes of Violence, the violent crime rate doubled between 1958 and 1968. Black workers and their families suffer the effects of crime almost three times more often than whites.
- Lower-middle-income workers often live close to those who receive government aid. A steady worker whose paycheck does not reach far enough, whose worklife is

less than optimal, and whose home environment is both drab and frightening, understandably may view with some resentment the use of his tax dollars to help his nonworking neighbor rather than himself out of a squeeze.

— In addition, many lower-middle-income workers, quite justifiably, feel that society does not prize the kind of work they perform. Our culture dramatizes diploma-accredited professionals but neglects skilled and un-skilled workers who transform ideas into tangible goods and services. The result is that young people look on many of the jobs in the $5,000 to $10,000 bracket as jobs of last resort; fathers hesitate to describe their jobs to their sons and hope to find, if not for themselves, at least for their children, another way to make a living.

In short, at home and at work, these people are living in a mine field. They are overwhelmed with problems and their dissatisfaction is expressed in workplace conduct that impacts negatively on productivity and increases employers' costs. The behavior and list of economic penalties are well known to all of us:

— work that is poor in quality and inadequate in quantity
— increased tardiness, absenteeism and work-injuries
— energy-sapping moonlighting
— higher turnover — stimulated by the endless search for a better break
— excessive wage demands in the futile effort to beat inflation
— mounting grievances that can lead to strikes and the complete rupture of production.

The problem is familiar, but what is the solution?

Within our well-established labor-management system we can do a number of things in the constructive interest of both workers and industry — if both management and labor square-ly face up to the pressures that impinge on the productivity of lower-middle-income workers and look for ways to relieve these pressures.

There are certain specific areas that should be examined for solutions:

The organization of work. Phrases such as job enrichment, job ladders, job redesign, and participation have been cheapened and therefore often discarded. Yet, the fact remains that full-scale job enrichment with a real commitment from management has produced remarkable results in the pioneering plants that have tried it.

Opportunities for advancement. Building wage and salary plans will not alone alleviate worker dissatisfaction. They must be supported by promotion policies that work at the lower levels of the organization at least as well as they do at middle and top levels.

Upgrading is a key way to help workers advance and to draw on untapped worker capabilities. By opening an avenue of progress and hope, upgrading stimulates individual effort. Workers desire opportunity to learn and advance more than any other single thing.

Adult vocational education can be an important tool in opening up advancement opportunities. Local community efforts in cooperative education offer exciting prospects to educators, businessmen and government officials. Company assistance for additional education, such as tuition-refund programs and leaves of absence, should aim at lower-middle-income employees as well as Ph.D.'s.

Incentive systems. Such systems have been receiving increased attention for middle management and executives, but seem to be declining at the lower levels. Too few companies have considered profit sharing or the highly effective Scanlon Plan, which shares cost reductions brought about through participation by workers, union and management in overall productivity improvement.

Supervisory training. Dissatisfaction with treatment *by* supervisors has been reported as one of the major blue collar complaints. Supervisors are the management in the eyes of the worker, like it or not. How first-line supervisors relate to subordinates or handle grievances reflects on management. Industries whose supervisors are not sensitive to the changing expectations of the oncoming generation and its demand to take part in decision-making can look for growing problems in their plants in the 1970's.

Occupational health and safety. Industry needs to take a close look at this both in terms of worker protection on the job and the adequacy of sickness and accident benefits.

The rate of disabling work-related injuries has increased more than 20 percent since 1958. Industrial accidents kill 14,000 persons each year; disable over 2 million; and account for 245 million lost man-days — five times the number of days lost from strikes. The landmark Occupational Safety and Health Act provides the instrument for an urgently needed cooperative effort among industry, labor and government to reverse these tragic statistics and promote human and economic welfare.

The fact that most blue collar workers lose at least a part of their income if they are disabled, brings into question the level and extent of sickness and accident benefits. Are waiting periods too long? Benefits too low? State governments should be encouraged to liberalize workmen's compensation. An analysis of the cost of these benefits will often show they are quite low in relation to the worker's value to the firm.

Employee thrift plans offer a very attractive method for easing the economic squeeze on workers. Under an employee thrift plan, costs can be fixed and benefits can be multiplied both to the firm and to the worker. If employer and employee contribute regularly by payroll deduction formula, the employee begins to accumulate a small and steadily growing account.

Other valuable features can include a low interest loan program, self-insured with a life insurance feature; withdrawal privileges without eroding all of the savings, and even long-term housing loans. Savings plans provide a balance wheel so that workers can draw upon these sources when their living costs are at a peak without incurring excessive interest charges or debts. Thrift plans also provide income for workers at retirement and protect families in case of death or disability.

Pension systems need review. About half of the 30 million American workers covered by private pension plans will never draw a penny in benefits. The reason, of course, is that pension benefits are forfeited when workers change jobs before retirement or before earning a nonforfeitable right — a vested pension.

Working wives can be an asset to both industry and the worker — if certain adjustments are made.

There are two ways that industry can employ women to its greater advantage. One is to increase the number of part-time jobs which are not only more compatible to the life-style of working wives with school-age children, but may reduce the inferior production caused by full-time work on a repetitive task. The other is to improve or provide child care arrangements. The fact is that in the United States good child care is difficult to find and make-shift arrangements affect productivity.

British experience indicates that productivity bargaining offers an excellent route by which to explore some of these suggestions.

Productivity bargaining has evolved as a realistic means of combining efficiency with economic advances for the worker. Generally, the results of this type of bargaining are beneficial. One in-depth study of 40 companies by the British National Board for Prices and Incomes shows that three-fourths of the companies achieved lower unit costs or deductions in total labor costs.

Productivity bargaining is still an underdeveloped art in the U.S. It should be used more. I am not suggesting it as a quick or easy solution. In fact, successful productivity bargaining is complicated and requires dedication to certain concepts:

1. The worker must know that his security is protected. No worker is going to accept a technological change that simply puts him out of a job. He may accept eventual displacement if the conditions of that displacement include an adequate buy-out: security for his old age, or a smooth transition to another job.

2. The bargaining must take place through existing institutional arrangements. It must recognize the role of unions and managers and the growing eagerness of

workers for greater participation in decision-making at the workplace.

3. There must be real commitment by top management to the idea that worker satisfaction is essential to increase productivity. All of us say this. But too often, I fear, our actions as managers indicate that we are more concerned with the machines than the men and women who operate them.

4. And finally, we must recognize that success requires long-term, consistent efforts. We can't do it all in one contract or one year. We must be willing to accept disappointment, to return to try again — and to have a lasting commitment to the goal.

After all, we are talking about changing human behavior. And what must change — with both managers and workers — are attitudes and behavior — neither of which can be reordered through simple directives from the executive suite.

Motivation to work and produce depends on the human spirit. This life force responds best to promise for personal achievement.

When life seems to be a closed-loop system of economic pressure, job dissatisfaction and community problems, then performance as a worker, as a citizen and as a person suffers. Workers who run the daily rat race on a muddy track, and are also-rans, can't be inspired to win.

The employer concerned with morale and motivation as adjuncts to strong profit-results needs to increase his awareness of the interplay between job performance and human expectations. Before an employer can effect real and lasting changes he must know the degree and nature of the problem in his specific workforce.

The nature of the job itself is intertwined with a man, his family, his life, his accomplishment, his status and his outlook on society. This dynamic interaction of the world of work with the life-style of the worker is a fact.

Economic rewards, personal job satisfaction and future opportunity are three basic elements that turn people on. Failure and frustration turn them off.

The future productivity of our society and its capacity to make a better world and a better America rest upon our ability to provide a better opportunity for more people. In the final analysis this involves the workplace more than any other single element.

Beyond Boredom: A Look at What's New on the Assembly Line

by Daniel Zwerdling

Until AT&T's "Work Itself" program came to North Virginia Bell two years ago, operator Mary Fiala had to raise her hand every time she needed to go to the bathroom. "This used to irritate the girls — oh, they just hated it," she says. But now, explained regional manager Charles Pfautz, "We tell them, 'Get up from the switchboard and go by yourself.' " In the old days, operators passed emergency calls to their supervisors — now they can handle the calls themselves. Operators now keep their own attendance records, and when answering calls they no longer have to use canned phrases. They can "say it like it is."

"What we're talking about here is a complete change," said Pfautz, "the employees managing themselves instead of being managed." Work Itself, says Mary Fiala, "makes it just a little bit easier to work here."

AT&T's "humanizing work" is a vague concept which has mushroomed in just two years from the theories of social scientists into one of the most vaunted — and volatile — work issues in years. It grows from the notion that much work is now inhuman — boring, monotonous, stiflingly rigid — and that many American workers are dissatisfied with the quality of their working lives. The HEW report, *Work in America,* suggests that to bring contentment and psychological well-being, companies must redesign jobs so workers no longer feel like soulless cogs in a vast corporate machine.

Two years ago scarcely anybody had heard of humaniza-

Reprinted with permission from *The Washington Monthly*. Copyright © 1973 by The Washington Monthly Co., 1028 Conn. Ave., N.W., Washington, D.C.

tion of work, but now it's a social fad. The subject has appeared as a *Newsweek* cover story, as a documentary on NBC's *First Tuesday,* and as massive research grants from the Ford Foundation — all barometers of social acceptance. The Productivity Commission is giving grants to major corporations and unions who want to redesign jobs to improve the quality of work. Humanization of work celebrated its big debut in March 1973. 250 executives gathered in the chandeliered splendor of the New York Hilton to hear a dozen companies including Chase Manhattan, AT&T, and General Foods, testify how *they* have humanized work. Senators Ted Kennedy and Charles Percy delivered the keynote speeches. The issue is clearly hot politics.

But behind this PR veneer the corporations, the government, and the unions are scared. When the HEW report was published, the White House tried to freeze it with silence, and Labor Department officials hoped that "if we'd all stop writing about the problem it would go away." While some companies are displaying their humanization of work programs like a United Givers Fund button (*I* humanized work), most of the 100 or so corporations conducting experiments are keeping them secret. A top United Automobile Workers official confided that the UAW "has dozens of experiments going with General Motors," but he added sharply, "This information is not for public consumption, understand? This conversation did not take place."

This conflict of emotions suggests that humanization of work is much more than a simple reformist movement. If the corporations play the right game, they hope, humanization of work will provide the key to greater profits: workers will be contented, toil harder, and never go on strike. Productivity will soar. But if they lose control, the corporations fear, the humanization movement could "open a Pandora's box from which there's no return," as Edwin Mills, director of the U. S. Productivity Commission's Quality of Work program explained. "Pretty soon you'll have the workers managing the managers. It's a first step toward encroaching on management's prerogative of controlling and directing the means of production."

The workers stand to gain substantially from the humanization of work movement — but only if they, and the unions, shape the issue as just one element in a long-range strategy for achieving increased workers' rights and control. So far, management has taken all the initiative and talks about humanization of work like some technological fix that can simply be installed on the production floor. . . .

The business world knows, deep in its boardrooms, that it faces a profound crisis. Bureau of Labor statistics show that absenteeism has soared 35 per cent since 1961 and annual turnover in the auto industry, for one, has topped 100 per cent (costing General Motors at least $79 million per year, according to a company bulletin). An increasing degree of sabotage is costly (General Foods dumped a huge batch of dog food when it came out green one day), and so is the use of drugs (15 per cent of the members of a UAW local surveyed at random take heroin). *"The best advice is this,"* the conservative Research Institute of America advises executives, "accept malaise as a fact." As the Corning Corporation's behavioral psychologist Michael Beers warns, "unless the initiative is taken by management, the risk of more chronic and less profitable change will be increased."

Each company which says it is humanizing work develops its own interpretations of what "humanizing" means. The New York banks and insurance companies, for example, are embracing "job enrichment" in their white-collar factories, where pools of labor — mostly women and minorities — have for years churned out paper forms like parts on an assembly line. Their actual work hasn't changed, but management has distributed it differently among the workers so each one takes on a more varied and less disjointed set of responsibilities. At Bankers Trust, a single stock transfer once passed through the hands of six different workers: one received the order, one typed it, one keypunched it, one checked it — on and on. The new, more individualized work flow is supposed to give them a feeling of ownership and expanded responsibility.

Other companies are tinkering a bit more with the way the work is actually done. Ford Motor, for example, lets workers — only 18 of them — assemble dashboard units for low volume, luxury-line cars on their own. General Motors is experimenting with a team-assembly approach in its new mobile homes. All these projects involve piecemeal changes here and there in the production process — as at Ford, one corner of a room can be "humanized" while the system is not.

But the biggest changes so far have come through the "socio-technical" approach. The company designs a system to promote a sense of worker autonomy and involvement from the ground up. The socio-technical system par excellence is General Foods' dog food plant in Topeka, Kansas. It starts operating the moment workers arrive at work: same parking lot for managers and workers, same entrance adorned with a beautiful mural, same decor in the management and production crew cafeterias. Workers have locker rooms with showers and carpets and ping-pong tables to encourage them to spend more time together and talk about work. Production teams of about eight workers each meet 15 minutes before and after their shift every day to plan who will do what job and talk about production problems with their "team leader" — their supervisor.

When salesmen come peddling new equipment, the management sends them to workers on the team who decide whether the gadgets will do the job. "I talked with one salesman who had an awful time," said Michael Brimm, a Harvard Business School student who worked in the plant for six months. "His boss couldn't believe he was talking only with the *workers*."

To most businessmen, all this is radical stuff. The norm in business is so rigid that even the most minute changes simulate a revolution. "I hope I don't sound like a radical," worried Chester Gray, the pin-striped and short-cropped commercial services manager for Washington, D.C., area Bell, after telling me about his "job enrichment" innovations, which include letting his employees cut off service to delinquent customers on their own initiative and take company files home at night. . . .

As the workers take over more and more of the small responsibilities the management used to exercise, middle managers feel their own limited powers sapped. Imagine the supervisor in an AT&T operators' office: struggled hard, worked for the company maybe 10 years, and now at the height of power, tells operators when they may or may not go to the bathroom, taps their lines to judge their performance, and records their every minute's absence. Suddenly, Work Itself comes and those powers vanish.

It's easy to understand management resistance. But *unions* are also resisting work redesign — perplexing and frustrating the humanization of work advocates. Here are social scientists promoting a movement designed to free workers — psychologically speaking, anyway — and they find the unions blocking the path.

Labor leaders have forever been wary of programs which somehow blur the distinction between management and workers, apparently even if it means nothing more than workers deciding when to take their breaks instead of depending on supervisors to tell them. This view was outlined for me by UAW committeeman Red Campbell from GM's Truck and Coach plant. First he complained that GM doesn't know what it's doing and is botching up the mobile home plant; but when I asked him whether workers should assume more managerial responsibilities in running the plant he became indignant. "We don't want a goddamn thing to do with management," he said. "If we're taking part in management, who the hell will we be fighting against? We don't want to be part of management's job. Our job is to see they do their job right."

Union leaders fear job redesign which increases worker power partly because they *don't want* the workers to have more power. The unions see threats to their own power in the humanization of work movement, or any movement which expands worker autonomy, just as their management counterparts do. If workers can make decisions at work they may also more actively question union policy. If they can replace management functions, why not replace functions of the union leaders? The rebellious mood among young workers which is shaking factories is also shaking the union structure. As far as the workers can see, management is doing something to make work more tolerable, while the unions just haven't delivered.

Unions are failing their memberships because they've settled into a rut. Management decides what to produce and how to produce it and whom to hire to produce it, and the unions fight for tangible rewards — pay, leave, financial benefits — in return. But humanizing the working place demands some new kinds of goals — autonomy, responsibility, a say in production methods. But this is foreign territory, and the unions don't feel comfortable traveling in it.

They don't know what to do about humanizing work, largely because they haven't spent much time or energy trying to figure it out.

The UAW and a few other unions will raise the humanization of work issue in future negotiations, but they're doing it reluctantly, and then only because management is forcing them to play their hand. "If General Motors wants to experiment, we have to be a part of that experiment," said a top UAW official. "We don't want them going over our heads and violating workers."

The unions have some sound instincts which make them leery of humanization of work programs — management can use them to co-opt workers — but they're following these instincts in the wrong direction. If the union leaders are really concerned about the well-being and security of their members, they should be plunging into the humanization issue, hashing out a sound strategy with the workers, and negotiating hard with management. That's the only way humanizing work can deliver worker benefits. Instead, the unions are condemning the movement and retreating from it like ostriches with their heads in the sand. By abandoning the workers, the unions guarantee precisely the result they say they fear — that management will manipulate it for its own gains.

While corporations have been forced to pacify their workers, to reduce absenteeism, high turnover, and sabotage, they have been feeling the pressure of foreign competition. And so the real dilemma, the Research Institute of America explains to executives, "is the need to push for higher productivity at a time when employees are waking up to a new feeling about themselves." Humanizing work has provided an answer. In the Productivity Commission's *Quality of Work* brochure, you won't see any mention of employee satisfaction for its own sake — but the brochure, which is sent to corporate executives, does promise that work redesign will bring "increased employee motivation and allegiance to union and company," the benefits of "decreased work place costs," and "improved utilization of human and technological resources."

"The key to the quality of work program," according to Edgar Mills, the director of the Productivity Commission, "is its principal national objective . . . measurably increasing American productivity, achieved not through speed-up but through new personal employee motivation."

Industry's temptation, as the unions say, is to buy a palliative which will expand sales and profits first and soothe production workers second. Private consulting firms peddle humanization of work plans like laxatives — take a spoonful when your system isn't working as it should. Roy Walters and Associates, a booming New York management consulting firm, packages a "job enrichment model" specially for banks and insurance firms: "Works relatively quickly," the ads boast, "not so long as to try the patience of management."

This slick, manipulative approach is precisely what many corporations like AT&T have engineered for their pathetically grateful employees today.

The small freedoms and decision-making powers that companies like AT&T have granted do make work more bearable, but only because it was so unbearable before. "It's all relative," said Charles Pfautz, the Bell manager who brought Work Itself to Northern Virginia. "An operator's job is more meaningful than it was, but it's still pretty awful."

Some corporations, it's true, have managed to restructure their jobs to make working there relatively pleasant. By convincing employees they have a stake in the business, bringing them into their confidence and giving them responsibilities which managers used to have, these companies have created a climate in which workers begin to think and act like management. Workers at Corning labor overtime not so much to get the time and a half, one woman told me, as because "we know what our production schedules are — and we know that we have to produce." The employees have the "freedom" to make changes in their work methods, if the changes increase the efficiency. "Workers can make their own decisions, as long as they make the decision management would have made for them," said a former employee of the Topeka plant.

The new loyalty and sense of ownership the workers feel toward their jobs which spurs them to work harder and better is ultimately a massive deception. The companies are not the workers' companies, the products are not their products, the jobs are not their jobs — and for every extra boost in production someone else is raking off the profits. Increased satisfaction on the job is important, but it's not enough; to be equitable, as a start, the corporations must share with the workers whatever extra profits their labors bring.

Many union leaders have been insisting all along that the work redesign issue has been a false one from the beginning — a creation of the intellectuals which the workers have never asked for and may not even want. Money is what counts. If the management really wants a happy work force, let them put their money where their mouth is and hand over some of the profits.

"I've been going around to all the Chrysler plants," UAW Vice President Doug Fraser told me. "We have 110,000 workers, and at all the locals I've visited not one worker raised the [humanization of work] problem with me — I mean not one single worker has come up to me and said, 'Why don't we do this work differently?'" James Wright, director of the New Unionists of the Movement for Economic Justice in Washington, D. C., said, "If you walked into the factory and asked workers 'What do you want to change around here?' I'm sure redesigning jobs is not going to be one of the first things they'll tell you."

Wright makes an important point: factory workers still confront the problem of day-to-day survival. At least 14,000 people die on the job each year, and perhaps 100,000 more die from "occupationally-caused diseases." In GM's assembly plant in Baltimore job redesign could hardly make a difference: after two hours I became violently headachy and nauseated from the noise and fumes.

But it doesn't make any sense to pit physical security against psychological security and weigh which is more important. That's not the point. The one issue that takes both into account and goes beyond is the question of who controls the safety policies and work redesign programs. Workers now exert no control over either. They get what the management can be made to give them.

If the work force — and the unions — are going to turn the humanization of work movement to their benefit, they must develop a long-range strategy rather than stumble on work redesign as managements arbitrarily present experiments. "When real change happens, it doesn't happen by someone else's design," argued James Wright. "When we talk about quality of work, well, whose work are we talking about? Workers'. Change on the job has got to begin on the bottom."

One effect of the corporate stranglehold is that employees — and management too — cannot conceive that the system could be any different.

Doug Fraser at the UAW, for example, can't imagine that the auto industry will ever assemble cars in a team — a method which both SAAB and Volvo in Sweden use to break the monotony and isolation of auto factories. In Sweden, cars roll off the line considerably slower than in American plants. "How the hell are we going to produce 60 cars an hour on a team?" Fraser asked. He begs the real question: who says we need to produce 60 cars an hour (101.6 at the Lordstown plant)? Who decided we needed to produce 9.3 million automobiles in America last year? It's a matter of priorities.

The answer to these questions transcends technological issues and becomes fundamental politics. The auto industries could produce cars by teams if they wanted — their decision to reject that route is governed strictly by far-reaching political and economic choice.

What the unions do with the humanization of work movement will largely determine whether the movement starts breaking down the work dictatorships which govern 82 million Americans each day — whether a workers' democracy will be built or whether the movement fizzles and brings what the Swedes call "toilet democracy" — AT&T at its very best.

If production workers begin to realize the system can work differently, and a workers' control strategy evolves, workers could negotiate for the right to decide on work redesign, and next for the right to exert controls over company safety policies. Workers can organize to gain influence over hiring and firing policies — without this even the most dramatic changes in humanized plants look ultimately meaningless. Work schedules, shifts, overtime, shutdowns — all these are issues which profoundly affect people's life at work. Unless the humanization of work movement encompasses these issues, too, it will all amount to very little.

Why Motivation Theory Doesn't Work

by Thomas H. Fitzgerald

Rising costs and recessionary pressures have prompted the business community, as well as administrators of public agencies, to seek economies. One potential source of savings is in labor costs, but these have resisted reduction because of the downward rigidity of wage rates and the difficulties of increasing aggregate labor productivity. The growing pressures for economy and productivity also stress other labor problems that increase costs: absenteeism and turnover, idleness and featherbedding, product defects and errors. All this is reflected in one of the more familiar questions one hears at management seminars, "How can I motivate my employees?"

Equally familiar to most of us are the recurring themes concerning the motivation problem developed by perhaps a score of business theorists and commentators. Their speeches and publications, together with a number of widely distributed educational films summarizing their views, have arrived at a common core of mid-range theory. What this theory says about employee motivation, both in diagnosis and prescription, is a significant advance from naive conceptions of "morale" during the World War II era, the discredited industrial engineering approach prior to that, and the casual omniscience of the popular press. But what, really, does it tell us?

Briefly, we are told that the concept of motivation is complex, but can and should be understood. Humans have

Reprinted with permission from *Harvard Business Review*, July-August 1971. Copyright © 1971 by the President and Fellows of Harvard College; all rights reserved.

basic physiological needs that must be satisfied, but these are supplemented by numerous other biosocial and culturally derived needs. The individual's actual movement to satisfy his needs depends not only on their state of readiness within himself but also on the objective situation in which he moves (i.e., the field containing other actors), together with his perception of the situation, which is in turn influenced by his own past experiences — i.e., successes or failures in finding satisfaction.

In the business environment, exchanging time for money may take care of a few of the worker's important needs, but it does nothing for those other "higher" needs such as sense of competence, recognition, and so on, that emerge after he has achieved a minimum amount of security. But the work must be performed in any case, and its failure to fill these higher needs results in frustration, antagonism, indolence, and malingering.

When motivation is found thus failing, management's response may not be to throw out the carrot-and-stick theory but to conclude either: (a) that work is inherently irksome and new and more interesting carrots are required, or (b) that workers are a shiftless and lazy lot and stronger sticks are required. The first conclusion, of course, has not solved the problem, while the second is self-validating and defeatist, and leads to more controls, more resentment, more "shiftless" behavior.

What can be done? The advice of the motivator fraternity shows a remarkable unanimity and, with some minor injustice to the subtlety of individual perception and diagnosis, can be summarized in the following three counsels:

1. Enlarge or enrich jobs to make the work more interesting by restoring challenge and the potential for achievement satisfactions. Employees will be motivated to perform well those tasks that are in themselves worth doing.

2. Institute training to modify supervisory style. Supervisors are encouraged to be employee-centered and to assist workers in defining and reaching their job goals. They should act as friendly helpers rather than as policemen.

3. Foster employee "participation" by encouraging work-

ers to take part in the decision process. Participation ranges from such elementary forms as giving employees advance notice of changes or explanations of these changes to more involved forms like stating a problem and requesting employee solutions. The final phase, still largely conceptual, is for the employees themselves to identify the problems, discuss possible solutions, and then arrive at joint decisions. Under these conditions, relationships would no longer be superior/subordinate or master/menial, hence characterized by antagonism and anxiety; instead, they would reflect a refreshing mutuality, trust, honesty, and concern in a climate where organizational goals coalesce with individual goals.

My purpose in this paper is to express doubts about these counsels and to suggest that their general adoption will be more difficult than anyone has recognized publicly. This is not meant to imply that the counselors claim general solutions; they admit difficulties and limitations and the fact that positive motivation in some situations, such as conventional assembly lines, is remote. But their writings, films, and public addresses have an unmistakable hortatory character and require a reasoned demurrer.

My thesis is that the proposed remedies are not adequate because the seriousness of the motivation problem has been underestimated. In what follows, I shall examine some early developments in the organization of rationalized work systems which, from the perspective of contemporary society, reflect assumptions that have become increasingly less valid and at the same time generate extensive tensions and strains. After discussing the advice commonly prescribed to mitigate this distress (the three counsels mentioned earlier), I shall offer some prescriptions of my own.

The problem of employee motivation has its origins in certain fundamental conditions of industrial society, and is magnified by the cumulative effect of historical and cultural trends. The roots of the problem are implicit in three early assumptions in the organization of rationalized work systems and will require more extensive changes in our interdependent, multi-dimensional systems than most businessmen, motivational theorists, and consultants would like to think.

1. STOPWATCH MEASUREMENT

An early assumption of the factory system involved the choice of a time frame in which certain utilitarian calculations were made. Since workers were paid a daily or hourly wage, the value of their output was computed on the same basis, while the use of the stopwatch made it possible to calculate output-value minute by minute, thereby firmly establishing utility in the short run. Production operations were rationalized to maximize output in this short run through detailed process planning and narrow division of tasks. This system simplified the tabulation of worker outputs and allowed effective control of large quantities of unskilled labor, but let us consider some of its other effects:

— The imperatives of short-run efficiency disrupted work group solidarities, and, simultaneously, the mass employment system and the extensive size of the plants hindered their formation; thus an important source of day-to-day, small group control of individual deviance was weakened, and the transmission and continuity of those values that make up the workmanship ethic were obstructed.

— Decisions on the quality of workmanship made by individual workers in the handicraft era were largely replaced by machine process control, which was made necessary in any case by the utilities of standardization and of interchangeability of parts.

— The vast elaboration of structure, together with the separation and, later, remoteness of ownership from management made it more difficult to identify with, or even see, the patrons of one's efforts.

It is scarcely now disputed that these dysfunctional consequences and the miscalculation of their real costs in a longer time frame are expressed in workplace problems such as employee hostility or indifference and unthinking dependency. What is important here, however, is that a narrow division of labor, churning of labor markets, and large-scale units are intrinsic parts of rationalized production systems where costs are computed in the short run (i.e., "false maximization"). Any attempt to resolve worker and workplace problems must recognize these structural sources.

2. OBJECTIVE DECISION MAKING

Another assumption of rationalized production has to do with what might be called the "spatial" frame; that is, the failure to foresee a widening of rational attitudes to the work force. As rationality became characteristic not only of production operations, but of engineering, investment, marketing, and management generally, calculation of objective inputs and outputs became the habitual basis for decisions. The broader effects of these decisions, however, as well as the cognitive style of the decision maker, could not long go unnoticed within the company. Difficulties arose when the same rational habits of mind infected the work force, displacing existing class and ethnic styles or causing doubts about the continuance of an earlier patrimonial solicitude.

However, the problem becomes more complicated when everyone decides to base the application of his efforts on pleasure-pain, input-output calculations as do utilitarian managers. This is especially true if, as is now the case, schedules of rewards are truncated by single rate pay systems and uniform work standards, while schedules of punishments are partly neutralized by a full employment-welfare system and the protection possible for individuals through combination (unions). Workers are transformed into job itinerants who do not identify with any one employer; the "rational" worker can blandly ask, "What's in it for me?"

But there is a further infection: that is to say, the spread of "competitive" attitudes to the managers and supervisors of the work force. The ethos of competition — of one against all, of individual maximization — belongs, properly speaking, to entrepreneurs and among entrepreneurs. When it spills over into the work force (or is even cultivated there by management that naively asserts it as a general good), it leads to a self-perpetuating cycle of suspiciousness, blaming and reprisals, withholding of information — either bad news or necessary facts — errors, defensiveness, and more distrust (although admittedly, one hears less of that competitive bravado with the growth of a systems approach to management).

3. *RIGID VALUE SYSTEM*

Perhaps the most important assumption concerns the availability of certain *nonrational* elements necessary to the work force, and implicit in the operation of rational organization as we know it. That is to say, the personality traits and values (orderliness, accuracy, neatness, punctuality, specialization of knowledge in a career path, success striving, deference to rank and authority, predictability, impersonality, reliance on rules and procedures, etc.) that "fitted into" the needs of rational bureaucracy so well, were not seen as possible *variables* but as a natural, continuing "given" — as was the society that bred these traits, the culture which was saturated with them.

Clear evidence to the contrary, of course, existed in anthropological reports of other societies in remote places, but now such evidence is widely available here in our own society. The lack of a temperament impelled toward assiduous effort or habitual striving for ever higher goals and the incomplete internalization of certain ascetic values and normative controls appear not only as an "exception" among ghetto blacks (who explicitly reject them) or the alienated white youth in the street culture, but increasingly in other sectors of society as well.

That there is now a widespread indifference to, or even contempt for, authority, both as "idea" and reality (ascribed status, deference, the legitimacy of externally imposed sanctions, tradition) has been widely reported. A persistent populism and egalitarianism, reinforced by the spread of empirical or "scientific" attitudes and demystification of "divine right," "natural law," and so on, seems to be responsible for the change. Professionalization of knowledge also increasingly strains against the authority of rank.

A further difficulty with this third assumption has been

noted by Charles Reich in his book, *The Greening of America*. He points out that the rising volume of industrial production, which is the inevitable result of successful, rationally organized enterprises, must be disposed of by means of a pervading and utopian advertising, which in turn is gradually disrupting industry's own foundation, the work force.

Workers, regularly instructed as consumers in a ceaseless acquisition of goods and services, lose their willingness to bear with the common drudgery. The offers of independence, the encouragement to self-aggrandizement, and the persistent flattery they experience as audience all contrast unfavorably with the discipline and the subordination which they experience as employees. Work loses its "religious" character, its centrality as the locus for the self. It is replaced by a sort of populist hedonism, ranging from compulsive accumulation to the new connoisseurship.

Even if consumption were not thus stimulated, human beings are not satisfied with constant rewards — unlike Professor Skinner's pigeons, one grain at $T_1 \neq$ one grain at T_n. The escalation of human wants, once satisfaction is achieved, produces a continuing problem. As workers "use up" their material shelter-survival needs, they seek such intangibles and unbuyables as freedom and autonomy (one might add, following Baudelaire: beauty, clarity, luxury, and calm). These, obviously, are incompatible with the life of organized production.

Questions seem to leap from a recognition of the increasing vulnerability of the foregoing assumptions, especially the third assumption. Will it be possible to continue to operate "efficient," closely synchronized, and interdependent organizations if change in the personality-culture system continues in the same direction? Put in another and more value-oriented way: How much personal freedom is *possible* in a hierarchical, bureaucratic authority system? At what point does individual style become incompatible with order?

To push it further, what is the potential for becoming an authentic self in a system characterized by well-defined role behaviors and role expectations that inherently demand reification and internalization?

Other questions, however, are at issue here: Are job enlargement, training, and employee participation realistic approaches to solving the new — as well as the old — motivation problem in industry? Are they practical? Will they work? It is to these counsels that we now turn.

Job enlargement is more modest than participation, less ambitious in its objectives, and apparently easier and less disruptive "to do." This prescription also has more substance than the talk therapies of the training-climate approach to motivation. While there is some empirical validation of the value of job enlargement, I am skeptical over its applicability in a wider variety of work situations and, more importantly, over a longer period of time.

There is probably little disagreement anymore about the desirability of eliminating as much as possible of egregiously repetitious operations, much as we correct poor lighting or dirty lavatories. In fact, in both shops and offices, a really repetitious job is an obvious candidate for automation or computerization. But after the more monotonous jobs are eliminated, we arrive at a wide range of operations where perception, rather than objective reality, is crucial.

Individuals differ vastly in their need for variety, responsibility, and competence, just as they vary in their need for independence or security. The job Jones finds moronic and insufferable is okay with Smith, yet too much for Brown. Restructuring and/or enlarging jobs are brave attempts to fit the job to the man, but *which* man? Do we have different sets and sequences of the same operations for people of varying competence, interest, and drive? Does turnover, then, imply continued rearrangement?

The school solution would reply: it's a matter for employment and placement to select similar people. But, of course, things don't work out that neatly in practice. Additional investments must also be made to broaden employee skills to meet increased responsibilities, although it is not yet clear whether employees will (a) expect greater compensation for this, or (b) be satisfied with increased psychic income.

It is obvious, however, that management's present flexibility in reallocating unskilled labor without loss of training investment would be reduced.

Finally, as time passes, one cannot but wonder how much of the added challenge remains, whether the broadened responsibility persists in its motivational propensity, or the worker merely paraphrases the well-known question, "What have you enlarged for me lately?" (How else to explain the faded motivation of those with amply challenging jobs — say, bored executives, doctors, or college professors?)

A second prescription for improved motivation — to enhance supervisory style and the climate of communication through in-house education and training — shares limitations similar to those cited for job enlargement: it does not get at enough of the basic incongruence between individual needs and organizational goals.

The fact that there is *some* congruence can be readily admitted, but this does not change the tension that exists anymore than does the recognition of the inconsistency of certain needs within the individual himself. The difficulty is that attention to improving attitudes and undesirable behaviors is usually directed at surface symptoms, without significant attempts to correct the underlying source. If a group of supervisors behave in a bossy, condescending, and insensitive manner, it is rarely because anyone *told* them to act that way, but because of other influences in the organization that are just as real as talk. For example:

— The system of selecting supervisors from the work group may make it clear that one type of personality will succeed, but others will not.

— Supervisory styles are perpetuated by modeling, and by the success of those who learn from the successful models. Attitudes about what is really important are conveyed not only by the official mottoes on posters, but in every conversation, in every inquiry and direction.

— An invidious system of monetary and status rewards must of necessity produce relative deprivation for some workers. The resulting competition to achieve rewards (or avoid deprivation) tends to encourage withholding of information and a lack of trust. Blaming, scapegoating, and defensiveness follow.

— Punishments and reprisals for deviance or poor performance in themselves provide satisfactions to those who have made the sacrifices necessary to self-discipline.

— Dependency is often cultivated at the lower levels because it is thought to ensure predictability of actions.

And so it goes. If we want to change all that, we have to ask (here, in behavioral terminology), "What are those forces in the situation that reinforce specific behaviors while acting to extinguish others?" Even where the supervisory attitudes themselves are found to be a cause of the motivation problem, change may be difficult because these attitudes are linked in with larger value systems — the belief that a supervisor should be dominant, assertive, even truculent, is supported by a more general mythology of masculine authority and prowess, and by a leadership imagery borrowed from athletics or the military.

Structural considerations: The failures of other attempts to change attitudes, as, for example, in efforts to eliminate racism in this country, have led to a reorientation of tactics of change toward more substantive methods; that is, to get inside "the black box" of institutional and organizational process. The lesson of that experience, however, is not necessarily that talk cannot change attitudes for the better, as well as encourage those who are ready to change. Some things are good in themselves, and a management that promotes a decent concern for employees' integrity, growth, and well-being should not have to look to an economic payoff as justification. The point here, however, is that education in itself has limited potential for producing and sustaining improvement unless changes, consistent with officially sponsored values, are also made in process and structure.

While participatory management is often urged by corporate liberals these days as the most desirable avenue of change, analysis of its dimensions and their implications for contemporary organizations suggests that it is questionable whether participation can correct pervasive apathy and indifference, let alone provide an unqualified good.

Of course, much of the advice is noble, urging the development of an improved climate of communication, trust, acceptance, mutuality, and so forth; but it is often unclear how, objectively, these attitudes are to be brought about and maintained. Also an open question is whether any significant percentage of the work force even wants to participate, other than perhaps for the novelty of doing so.* Although the advocates of this prescription for motivational health have failed to supply many important details of actual implementation, it is not hard to surmise what new difficulties might evolve.

Pressure for more involvement: Participation is not a simple or linear gradation of acts. It means more, for example, than giving accurate information, listening to responses, answering questions, seeking advice or ratification. It may mean interactions with groups of employees, as well as one-over-one relationships. The subjects of participation, moreover, are not necessarily restricted to those few matters that management considers to be of direct, personal interest to employees, or to those plans and decisions which will benefit from employee advice. Neither of these positions can be maintained for long without (a) being recognized by employees as manipulative or (b) leading to expectations for wider and more significant involvement — "Why do they only ask us about plans for painting the office and not about replacing this old equipment and rearranging the layout?"

Once competence is shown (or believed to have been shown) in, say, rearranging the work area, and after participation has become a conscious, officially sponsored activity, participators may very well want to go on to topics of job assignment, the allocation of rewards, or even the selection of leadership. In other words, management's present monopoly — on initiating participation, on the nomination of conferees, and on the limitation of legitimate areas for review — can in itself easily become a source of contention.

---

*See Robert Dahl, "The Case for Worker Control," *New York Review of Books,* November 19, 1970.

Potential for disruption: Another difficulty with partici- pation has to do with organizational effectiveness. The dysfunctions of bureaucratic systems are now well known, while the motivational potential of employee involvement is, if yet unrealized, at least widely anticipated. But the dysfunc- tional, disruptive effects of participation on rationally or- ganized systems should not be ignored either. Before embark- ing on participatory management, advocates should consider the following points:

— It is not at all clear how the highly variable competence of employee participants can contribute to the solutions of corporate problems that have specific technical constraints, even though these employees are affected by the results. As the store of knowledge expands (and becomes more opaque) along with the need for its accurate application, organiza- tions rely increasingly on experts and professionals, and it may in fact be true that the girls on the carton-folding opera- tion really have nothing to contribute to almost anything im- portant about running a container company. Once again, meritocracy confronts democracy.

— The scale of contemporary industry makes the impli- cations of decisions, and the interaction of their effects, hard to foresee, although the need for precision is now greater. At some point the "critical mass" of large organizations is reached where their manageability even by the few — much less the many — becomes questionable. The closely linked, synchronized, interdependent nature of the numerous sub- systems that now comprise large organizations would appear to make serious participation questionable not only in its technical aspects but in its goal-directed behavior. Inevitably, participation to any significant degree will cause indetermi- nacy and delay, loss of consistency and coherence, diluted and compromised objectives.

— Although it hasn't been discussed much yet, when blacks and women finally integrate supervisory and mid-man- agement ranks, they may coalesce into identity groupings to seek representation. We already have examples of teachers, college students, welfare recipients, and others who have been demanding the right to participate as groups to help de-

termine not only conditions within the system but its operation and outputs as well. Aside from the real costs in reduced
effectiveness (partly balanced, of course, by better motivation,
higher output, less waste, and so on) the impact of this new
participation on the process and structure of management,
though hard to estimate, must be anticipated, because what
is really involved is politics, the conscious sharing of control
and power. History does not offer many examples of oli-
garchies that have abdicated with grace and goodwill.

Once again, all this is not to imply that because gross
efficiency and productivity may be reduced, we should not
proceed toward alternatives. Given the goal of maximizing
utility, however, there does seem to be a necessary trade-off
between precision, on the one hand, and motivation through
participation, on the other hand, and we shouldn't assume
that we can have it both ways, just as we now admit that we
can't have both full employment and price stability. The
amount of each we want (or can tolerate), the location of the
best trade-off point, is a matter of experimentation and calculation. Viewed from a wider perspective, it is also entirely
possible for organizations to pursue new, multiple, even di-
vergent goals, although the trade-off problem then becomes
much tougher, involving basic values, or as they say these
days, "priorities."

It may be that the question, "How do I motivate my employees?" is not quite relevant to what is going on. Truth
is sometimes damaged in the process of analysis and recon-
struction, and concepts can easily become more "real" than
the reality from which they were cut. When transplanted from
the laboratory, the language of motivation may become subtly
elitist by suggesting that the employee resembles a captive
rodent in a training box equipped with levers, trick doors,
food pellets, and electric grids. Talking about a majority
(perhaps, in fact, a minority?) of people and how they live
as being "motivated" may provide only a pretentious terminology which deflects understanding.

When a man gets up in the morning, we can say this act
is a conditioned response to the stimulus of an alarm, but

that doesn't *tell* us anything important. To say he is motivated by hunger may be true, but perhaps he is not hungry and thinks instead, "Seven o'clock; *time to get up.*" What he does the rest of the day may have much the same toneless character of going from one thing to another and getting by. This may very well be the way it is for a great many people, at least during the time they spend in the shop or the office, because most of what they really care for is in other places and at other times. A few of them may not even care strongly for much of anything, almost anywhere. It is just possible that some whom we employ *can't* be motivated!

I am aware, following a critique such as this, of expectations for suggesting alternatives. They can be offered so as not to deny my wider meliorism; yet their statement should not distract from the main thrust of the argument presented here: the problem of employee motivation is rooted in certain fundamental conditions of industrial society, and its solution will require costly and extensive changes in our interdependent, closely linked systems. Just as most of the signs point to a pervasive consumerism, environmentalism, and governmental surveillance in the market economy, so we should anticipate a persistent alienation of industrial and business manpower in relation to its employers.

What can be done; what is being tried? At very little cost we can avoid giving offense or being intrusive. Merely talking with people also does a lot of good, although it does not seem to be easy for many managers. Here is a brief overview of other possibilities:

— Inexpensive means such as emblems, slogans, contests, and sets of monogrammed glasses function as attention getters, but their transference value is always speculative.

— Praise and approval can produce temporary improvement of individual effort.

— Company-sponsored recreation and house organs are also comparatively cheap and seem to have a positive effect on some of the people part of the time.

— Money is recurrently popular as an incentive for more and better work, but the general decline of piecework and profit-sharing plans testifies to the experience that these monetary incentives are not really effective in practice, due in part to intervening variables such as employee perception of an ambiguous means-ends relationship.

— Reducing the size of a productive or service unit seems to increase identification and improve motivation, but may introduce inefficiencies (especially as viewed by traditional costing methods) with no assurance of net gain.

— Stripping away the baroque elaborations of office may result in loss of the mystique of authority, but it could help create the conditions for unity.

Increasingly more expensive than the foregoing — in original investment as well as in maintenance — are mixes of "training" to improve skills and climate, of job enlargement, and of organizational development and participation. All imply substantial alterations in the way organizations are wired together and in communication and controls. They will eventually involve examination of reward and succession systems, priorities, and ends. Participation especially, as pointed out earlier, not only may start out as an unpleasant ride for those who are accustomed to being fully in charge, but also may become one from which it is increasingly hard to dismount.

What is needed is not merely the "willingness to confront change" (already a safe thought-cliché) but a commitment to go beyond changes in structure and procedures. What may even be required is relinquishing certain behaviors and beliefs, such as an ideology of certitude and constraint, a habit of objectifying people because of ranking or role ascription, or a style of address characterized by cant and bravado — difficult to give up, but not impossible.

We have seen progress in other areas where we once would not have expected it. We look back now at personality testing, slightly incredulous at its colonialist mentality and its banality of concepts, wondering how we could have been taken in by its promises of penetration and mastery. Similarly, perhaps yet in our time, we will be willing to discard the dismal vocabulary of motives, motivators, and motivation and start to think seriously about how to go about becoming a society of persons.

New Patterns for Working Time

by Janice Neipert Hedges

Long-term trends in working time have involved reductions in numbers — the number of hours worked per week, the number of workweeks in the year, or the number of years in the worklife. Recently, new arrangements or "patterns" of working time, with little or no change in total hours, have appeared in many industrialized nations.

These new patterns have stimulated widespread discussion of the merits of the old versus the new. Should workers, for example, work fewer but longer days? Should they, wherever possible, set their own schedule? Should the extended period of education that is concentrated in youth and the unbroken stretch of work in maturity be interspersed? And should retirement be a more gradual process?

What is being questioned is not so much the prevailing patterns of work, but rather whether their rigidity serves the interests of either a firm or its work force. At issue also is whether the work ethic can flourish in the midst of rigidity, in societies whose workers are well educated and have high standards of living.

The current challenge to standard and inflexible patterns of work is being pressed most actively in European nations that are experiencing labor shortages. Legislation and collective bargaining agreements pose fewer obstacles in many European countries than in the United States to experimenting with new arrangements in worktime.

International interest in new patterns for working time led the Organization for Economic Co-operation and Develop-

Reprinted with permission from *Monthly Labor Review*, February 1973, published by the U.S. Bureau of Labor Statistics.

ment (OECD) to sponsor a conference in Paris in September 1972 "to promote diversification and variability in the regulation and allocation of time for work, study, and leisure, under the highest possible freedom of individual choice." The delegates, who represented governments, workers, and employers from the 23 member countries agreed that a review of working time patterns should be undertaken. The growing tendency of workers in many countries to achieve flexibility through absenteeism lent urgency to their discussions.

In both North America and Europe, alternatives to standard full-time schedules are being sought. However, the new schedules seem to be taking different directions on the two continents. In the United States and Canada, the move has been toward a greater concentration of the amount of "time off" in a week. The "compressed workweek," illustrated by the 4-day, 40-hour schedule, was the forerunner of change.

In Europe, the move has been toward flexible workweeks, or "flexi-time," that change neither the total number of workdays nor the total hours required. Instead, workers are free to set their own arrival and departure times day by day, within certain limits.

In no country has either new workweek become the dominant pattern. The most extensive application is in Switzerland, where an estimated 15-20 percent of all industrial firms are on a flexible schedule. In Germany, the proportion of all workers on such workweeks is estimated at 2-3 percent, while the proportion of all full-time workers in the United States who are on 4-day schedules at present is estimated at less than one-half of 1 percent. However, because of the widespread expectation that these new workweeks will become prevalent in the future, it is useful to examine their origins and their impact.

Most of the impetus for the 4-day workweek in the United States has come from management, as a response to typical management concerns: to raise profits by increasing production and/or decreasing costs or to improve recruitment of skilled workers in short supply. Increased output is sought primarily by using shifts of 4-day workers to extend the hours that equipment is in operation or that customer service is available. Decreased costs are sought through improving productivity per man-hour by reducing startup and shutdown time, adjusting the supply of man-hours to workload patterns, reducing absenteeism and turnover, and improving worker morale.

Among other factors that may motivate management to consider a 4-day workweek is its potential for achieving other changes. For example, workers may agree to some evening and Saturday work in exchange for occasional 3-day weekends. And sometimes the major motivation is to improve the firm's image as a progressive, innovative company.

The consequences of 4-day schedules are at least as interesting as the objectives that lead management to their adoption. The famous Hawthorne experiments are a reminder of the need for caution, however, since few firms have had more than 2 years' experience with such schedules.* It also is well to remember that the failure rate of 4-day schedules has been estimated at 5-15 percent.

The benefits that frequently are reported for business are illustrated by an American Management Association study. Four-fifths of the 4-day firms in that study reported that a 4-day week "improves business results"; three-fifths indicated that production was up, almost two-fifths stated that costs were down, and half reported higher profits. Among the firms that did not experience positive benefits from their 4-day schedules, the proportion that reported that their production, cost, or profit situation remained about the same was far larger in each of these categories than the proportion that reported negative results.

The Bureau of Labor Statistics is conducting a pilot study of firms in various industries that have been on a 4-day schedule for a year or more. Early reports indicate that the objectives for adopting such a schedule generally were achieved, whether those objectives were extending the firms' hours, reducing paid overtime or other costs, reducing ab-

---

*The Hawthorne experiments concluded that gains in productivity over a period of years, which had been attributed to improvements in working conditions, had to be ascribed in the end to the workers' sense of involvement in a novel experience.

senteeism, improving efficiency, or enhancing the firm's image.

Not all the results for the firm are positive, however. Tardiness sometimes increases and scheduling may be a serious problem. Worker fatigue and its effects on output and work injuries over the long term are still an unknown factor.

What seem to be the consequences of 4-day workweeks for workers? The immediate results of 4-day schedules for workers have been reported: the concentration of leisure hours into an additional "free" day per week; a 20-percent reduction in commuter trips, saving both time and money; and possible economies in work-related expenses, such as child-care or restaurant meals. In addition, a reduction of 2 to 3 hours of work per week often accompanies the introduction of a 4-day week. However, not all the evidence is in. The effects of compressed workweeks for fatigue and family life are among the unresolved and crucial issues.

Fatigue was cited as a principal disadvantage of 4-day workweeks by only 8 of the 143 4-day firms in the American Management Association's study, half as many as cited more involved scheduling. Fatigue can be excessive to the point of endangering health, however, without coming to the immediate attention of management, since it does not necessarily affect injury rates or output.

Evidence that long workdays cause excessive fatigue was a major consideration in the adoption of 8-hour days. Labor organizations generally oppose any change in laws or collective bargaining agreements that would allow workdays of over 8 hours without overtime pay.

The physical strain of many jobs has been reduced in the years since the adoption of the 8-hour day, but mental and emotional stress may have increased. Fatigue varies from industry to industry and from job to job, depending on the exertion required and working conditions, such as heat and noise. It also varies by worker. (Contrary to expectations, some reports have indicated that younger workers, who are more likely to maintain their usual schedule of weeknight activities, are more fatigued by compressed schedules than older workers.) Over the long term, fatigue could be serious for many workers on compressed 4-day schedules of 9½- or 10-hour days plus commuting time.

What is the expected impact of the 4-day week on family life? Concern has been expressed by both management and labor organizations that compressed 4-day schedules will be particularly hard on women workers with families. Surveys of employees who have worked such schedules, however, seem to indicate that the majority of married women workers prefer schedules that give them a 3-day weekend in exchange for longer days. Perhaps women workers find that household work can be done more efficiently in the additional day off than in the fragmented time previously available before and after work. Or perhaps other family members assume more of the morning and evening work, with the result that the working wife's total workday is no longer than before.

In firms that use the 4-day schedule to extend their hours of operation, late shifts or rotating schedules that involve some weekend work often are adopted. Such schedules generally are considered to have detrimental effects on workers and families.

The results that compressed workweeks for either men or women workers have for their families cannot be gaged without further experience. The effect of sacrificing leisure time at the end (or beginning) of each workday in exchange for an additional day off, for example, depends on the use to which workers formerly put their daily hours of leisure and how they now use the full day of leisure. For those who use compressed schedules to take additional, part-time jobs, the result would be increased family income but less time together. The effect of the new workweeks on multiple job-holding, however, is another unknown at this time.

Beyond these issues are others that relate specifically to the "humanization" of work: issues, for example, of autonomy and democracy. In most firms where a new workweek is under consideration, employees participate in the decision. Their reactions generally are sought to a proposal for a trial period, and management, with rare exceptions, is ready to withdraw if the majority opposes the change. Some firms poll their employees on their individual preferences for days off, and their judgment on how nonwork days should be allocated: whether, for example, by rotating or seniority. After the completion of the experimental period, some firms again poll employees for their suggestions for further changes and in some cases for their opinions on whether the new work schedule has made a difference in the amount and quality of the work they produce.

Usually, though, the initiatives in work scheduling remain with management, with the employees' role confined to reacting to management's proposals and inquiries. Once a 4-day schedule is established on a permanent basis, the new schedule offers individual workers little voice in determining how many days they will work a week. Employees on a 5-day schedule in a firm where 4 days is the norm are at least as rare as 4-day workers in situations where the norm is 5 days. The new schedules enlarge the workweek options only for those workers who are able to change jobs or for workers looking for their first job.

European delegates to the recent OECD conference generally were critical of the concept of compressed workweeks because of the implication they saw in that concept that work is performed only for money and should be disposed of as expeditiously as possible. The general view was expressed by the director of the Central Union of Swiss Employers' Association: "Personally, I cannot get used to the idea that the worker must live for 4 whole days for work alone and for recuperating the strength he needs, while his cultural and social life, his human contacts in and outside the family, and his leisure time activities are pushed back and compressed into 2 weekdays and Sunday." The Europeans acknowledged, however, that the 4-day week must be evaluated in relation to weekly hours: The situation is different between a 44-hour week characteristic in many European countries and, for example, a 36-hour week. Nonetheless, Europeans are more interested in flexible schedules, or "flexi-time."

The essential provision of the flexible work schedule is that workers can, within a prescribed band of time in the morning and again in the afternoon, start and finish work at their discretion as long as they complete the total number of hours required for a given period, usually a month. That is, the workday can vary from day to day in its length as well as in the time that it begins and ends. The morning and evenings bands of time often are designated as "quiet time." Telephone calls and staff meetings are confined to "core time," which generally runs from midmorning to midafternoon. Time clocks or other mechanical controls for keeping track of the hours worked usually are a part of flexible workweek systems.

The primary force behind flexible workweeks in Europe, as with 4-day workweeks in North America, is management. Efficiency again is the major goal, but the efficiency of flexitime is related only to human resources.

Managers see flexible schedules as a means of recouping man-hour or fractions of man-hours that have been lost through erosion rather than through formal agreement. The situation of one of the first German firms to experiment with flexible schedules illustrates this erosion: Chronic traffic congestion made workers tardy, but the tight labor market ruled out disciplinary measures.

The firm realized, however, that traffic tie-ups were only one of the factors responsible for a growing deterioration in the ratio of man-hours worked to man-hours paid. In addition, workers required time for a variety of personal and family matters that could not always be accommodated to a rigid work schedule. They also realized that individual workers vary in their efficiency cycles, daily as well as monthly. Some are early risers who prefer to finish their work by midafternoon; others prefer a later schedule.

The developers of flexible scheduling believed that fewer man-hours would be lost if employees were given greater freedom in arranging their working time. The results of flexi-time seem to substantiate this confidence.

Flexible schedules are reported to result in an increase in the ratio of man-hours worked to man-hours paid. Part of the increase is due to the fact that time is no longer lost because of tardiness or short periods of unrecorded leave. In additions, many firms report that days absent decline. Sick leave is reduced because accumulated time credits, rather than "the monthly flu," can be used for personal affairs.

Hours worked also are reported to be more productive, resulting in less need for overtime work. Employees are likely to leave at a "stopping point" in their work, rather than slowing down as the end of the workday approaches. Moreover, they tend to leave early when work is slack, and to work later when work is heavy. The "quiet times," without telephone or other interruptions, are particularly productive for work that demands concentration. Moreover, employees are reported to be more receptive to changes in procedures and organization because of an improvement in the working climate.

Improved ability to recruit personnel also has played a part in the development and growth of flexible schedules. Their potential for drawing more of the native population, especially housewives, into the labor force is largely responsible for a growing interest in these schedules among some European governments, which have been experiencing severe and long-term shortages of labor and are concerned about their dependence on imported workers. Interest in reducing peak demands on transportation facilities also is a factor in some governments.

Flexible workweeks are not without their disadvantages for the firm. The hardware and administration of time-recording systems needed and extra utilities because of the firm's extended hours all involve costs. Having a particular worker available at any time outside core time is another problem. But many managers feel that with proper planning, flexibility can be reconciled with order, and efficiency can be increased.

For workers, the major benefit of flexi-time is the reduction in psychological and physiological stresses that follows from their right to make some adjustments in the timing of their work. Flexi-time may also help to democratize work. Flexible hours require more delegation of authority by supervisors. Moreover, they reduce the distinction between managers and professional workers, who have always been somewhat flexible in their working time, and other white-collar employees.

Flexible workweeks hold some disadvantages for workers, however. The need for time clocks or other time records, for example, seems to some observers the antithesis of democracy in the workplace, despite proponents' claims that controls for balancing out hours worked and hours required are not analogous to controls for tardiness. In some firms, the argument against time recording has been countered by including top management in the system. This has been more symbolic than real, however, since the records usually are not processed for top management. Another drawback of flexible schedules is that not all workers participate. Although flexitime may reduce distinctions among white-collar workers, many service workers and blue-collar workers in production jobs often are excluded. . . .

The case for introducing greater flexibility into lifetime patterns of work is similar to that for flexible workweek schedules: people are individuals who differ from one another in their needs and capabilities. Some prefer, for example, to complete their occupational preparation without a break, others profit more from education or training after some work experience, while still others learn their skills on the job. In regard to retirement, some workers want to retire early, some want to work full-time into old age, and some want to ease gradually into retirement. Edgar Faure, French Minister of State for Social Affairs (and former Prime Minister), recently spoke of the need to progress beyond the idea of "immutable categories" that control lifetime patterns of work. He criticized the division of life into "three ages of man": when people "study but do not work, . . . work and do not study at all, and finally . . . [are] supposed neither to work nor to study."

Patterns of education constitute an area of particular interest in many countries, as formal schooling and job training absorb larger segments of lifetimes. Experts have argued that new patterns of work and study will have to emerge as the concept of concentrating all education and training in an initial phase becomes outmoded. One pattern now under consideration would allow workers to alternate work and study periods even during initial post-secondary education and would include refresher courses at suitable intervals.

An increase in provisions for "early retirement" in some countries, including the United States, is one approach to increasing the ability of retirement systems to meet the capacity, desires, and circumstances of individuals. Other means of achieving flexible retirement patterns have also been suggested. Among these are removing maximum age limits in many cases, transferring older workers on request to less demanding jobs, and providing opportunities for temporary retirement or part-time work prior to and after normal retirement age.

11/09